THE INSTITUTE OF ECONOMICS

OF

THE BROOKINGS INSTITUTION

The Carnegie Corporation of New York in establishing the Institute of Economics declared:

"The Carnegie Corporation, in committing to the Trustees the administration of the endowment, over which the Corporation will have no control whatsoever, has in mind a single purpose—namely, that the Institute shall be conducted with the sole object of ascertaining the facts about current economic problems and of interpreting these facts for the people of the United States in the most simple and understandable form. The Institute shall be administered by its Trustees without regard to the special interests of any group in the body politic, whether political, social, or economic."

PUBLICATION NO. 52

For a full list of publications see the end of the volume.

THE BROOKINGS INSTITUTION

The Brookings Institution—Devoted to Public Service through Research and Training in the Social Sciences—was incorporated on December 8, 1927. Broadly stated, the Institution has two primary purposes: The first is to aid constructively in the development of sound national policies; and the second is to offer training of a super-graduate character to students of the social sciences. The Institution will maintain a series of co-operating institutes, equipped to carry out comprehensive and inter-related research projects.

The responsibility for the final determination of the Institution's policies and its program of work and for the administration of its endowment is vested in a self-perpetuating Board of Trustees. The Trustees have, however, defined their position with reference to the investigations conducted by the Institution in a by-law provision reading as follows: "The primary function of the Trustees is not to express their views upon the scientific investigations conducted by any division of the Institution, but only to make it possible for such scientific work to be done under the most favorable auspices." Major responsibility for "formulating general policies and co-ordinating the activities of the various divisions of the Institution" is vested in the President. The by-laws provide also that "there shall be an Advisory Council selected by the President from among the scientific staff of the Institution and representing the different divisions of the Institution."

CURRENT MONETARY
ISSUES

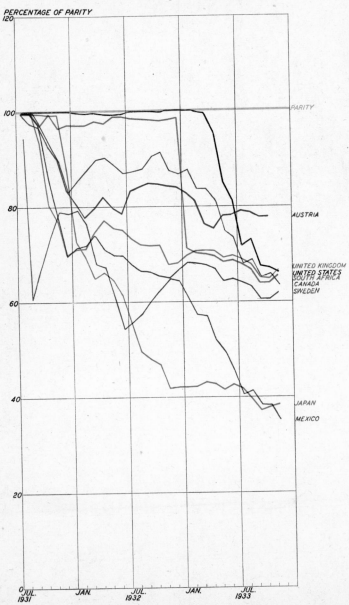

BREAKDOWN OF THE INTERNATIONAL MONETARY
SYSTEM, 1931-33
Average Monthly Ratios of Principal Depreciated
Currencies to Respective Gold Parities

CURRENT MONETARY ISSUES

BY

LEO PASVOLSKY

WASHINGTON, D. C.

THE BROOKINGS INSTITUTION

1933

Printed in the United States of America by
George Banta Publishing Company
Menasha, Wisconsin

Each investigation conducted under the auspices of The Brookings Institution is in a very real sense an institutional product. Before a suggested project is undertaken it is given thorough consideration, not only by the Director and the staff members of the Institute in whose field it lies, but also by the Advisory Council of The Brookings Institution, composed of the President, Institute Directors, and leading staff members. As soon as the project is approved, the investigation is placed under the supervision of a special committee consisting of the Director of the particular Institute in whose field it falls and two or more selected staff members.

It is the function of this committee to advise and counsel with the author in planning the analysis and to give such aid as may be possible in rendering the study worthy of publication. The committee may refuse to recommend its publication by the Institution, if the study turns out to be defective in literary form or if the analysis in general is not of a scholarly character. If, however, the work is admittedly of a scholarly character and yet members of the committee, after full discussion, cannot agree with the author on certain phases of the analysis, the study will be published in a form satisfactory to the author and the disagreeing committee member or members may, if they deem the matter of sufficient importance, contribute criticisms for publication as dissenting footnotes or as appendixes.

After the book is approved by the Institute for publication a digest of it is placed before the Advisory Council of The Brookings Institution. The Advisory Council does not undertake to revise or edit the manuscript, but each member is afforded an opportunity to criticize the analysis and, if so disposed, to prepare a dissenting opinion for publication in the volume.

DIRECTOR'S PREFACE

The year 1933 has witnessed the taking, either by legislative enactment or by executive order, of several steps which have profound significance for the monetary, banking, and fiscal future of our country. Some of these measures—for example, the so-called "Thomas amendment"—were merely permissive in character. Hence the precise nature of the changes which are being introduced into our financial system is to be discerned only in the light of unfolding events. It has seemed to the Institute of Economics, therefore, that great service in the understanding of developments and in the formulation of intelligent public opinion could be rendered through a series of current studies of these measures and of such lines of governmental action as emerge from them.

The present volume is the first result of such studies to be published. It undertakes to lay a foundation for the subsequent books and pamphlets in this series by presenting a general survey of the monetary issues which have dominated world economic discussions during the past year. After showing the divergence of opinion between various groups and nations participating in international discussions and negotiations during the course of the year, its sets forth the trend of monetary developments in the United States.

In view of the fact that monetary policy in this country is still in a state of flux, we believe that the presentation of this analysis at the present moment is peculiarly timely. Our ability to present the book now, however, is not the result of hurried work, but is due to the fact that researches in this field were begun by us a long time ago. For several years Mr. Pasvolsky has been devoting close study to the problem of the stabilization of the exchanges and other monetary developments in post-war Europe. For this purpose he has made two extended visits covering the principal countries of Europe and was at Geneva during the preparations for the World Monetary and Economic Conference and in London during the sessions of the conference. Upon his return to the United States it seemed wise not to defer any publication in this field until he could prepare a long and technical volume on the researches which he had been conducting. Instead we decided to bring those studies to a sharp focus at this time upon the immediate problem which is confronting the United States today in the form of a shorter and less technical treatment for a larger audience.

No effort is made in this small volume to pass judgment upon the whole range of specific monetary issues which now confront the world, or to suggest any specific program. We confine our attention here to indicating the vital relationship of present monetary policies to economic recovery. Other studies now under way in this series will deal more specifically with such problems as the following: The adequacy of the gold supply; the relation of unstable exchanges and devalued currencies to foreign trade and commodity prices; techniques and effects of foreign exchange control; and others.

This series is under the general supervision of Charles O. Hardy. Others who have served with the Director as a committee co-operating with the author in the preparation of this volume are Harold G. Moulton and Cleona Lewis. We have also had the aid of an advisory committee of the Social Science Research Council.

Edwin G. Nourse
Director

Institute of Economics
December 1933

CONTENTS

PAGE

DIRECTOR'S PREFACE ix
INTRODUCTION I

CHAPTER I

BREAKDOWN OF THE GOLD STANDARD 5
   I. Monetary Position of the World at the Beginning
      of 1933 7
  II. Outlook for Restoration of the Gold Standard . . 13

CHAPTER II

GENEVA: ADJUSTMENT OF CONFLICTING VIEWS 16
   I. The Gold Standard Issue 17
     A. Arguments for a Permanent Abandonment
       of Gold 18
     B. Arguments for Restoration of the Gold
       Standard 21
     C. The Geneva Line-Up 22
  II. Disagreement on Role of Commodity Prices 26
     A. Price Recovery as an Antecedent to Economic
       Recovery 27
     B. Price Recovery as an Accompaniment of
       Economic Recovery 28
  III. Experts' Recommendations 30

CHAPTER III

WASHINGTON: SHIFTS OF EMPHASIS 36
   I. America's Departure from the Gold Standard . . . 37
     A. Suspension of Gold Redemption and Exports 37
     B. Gold and Dollar Exchange Position 42
     C. Authorized Changes in Monetary Policy . . . 46
     D. Objectives and Control Provisions 52
  II. Washington Consultations 55
  III. Domestic versus International Program of Re-
      covery 60

CHAPTER IV

LONDON: CLASH OF POLICIES AND IMPASSE 64
   I. The Breakdown of Currency Truce Negotiations 66
  II. Resurgence of Price Controversy 70
     A. Debate on Credit and Prices 71
     B. Three Groups at the Conference 76
 III. President Roosevelt's Message to the Conference 80
 IV. The Impasse 85
  V. Results and Reports of the Conference 87

CHAPTER V

MONETARY POSITION SINCE THE LONDON CONFERENCE 92
   I. The Gold Bloc 93
  II. British Imperial Monetary Alliance 96
 III. Developments in the United States 99

CHAPTER VI

THE GOLD PURCHASE PLAN 107
   I. Theoretical Basis of the Plan 107
     A. The Price of Gold and the Price of Com-
       modities 108
     B. The Price-Raising Mechanism 110
     C. The Price-Stabilization Mechanism 113
  II. Efficacy of the Plan 115
     A. Experience of Six Countries 116
     B. The Complex Character of Price Adjustments 119

CHAPTER VII

THE TWO MAJOR ISSUES 127
   I. Implications of Monetary Uncertainty 128
  II. The Future of Monetary Organization 130

DOCUMENTARY APPENDIXES

APPENDIX A

MONETARY DISCUSSION IN THE ANNOTATED AGENDA 135

APPENDIX B

JOINT STATEMENTS ON WASHINGTON CONSULTATIONS 154
    I. American-British Statement 154
    II. American-French Statement 155
    III. American-Italian Statement 156

APPENDIX C

AMERICAN DECLARATIONS OF POLICY AT THE LONDON
    CONFERENCE 158
    I. Draft Resolution on Credit and Prices 158
    II. Draft Resolution on Restoration of the Gold
        Standard 159
    III. Official Statement Relative to President Roose-
        velt's Message to the Conference 160

APPENDIX D

BRITISH DECLARATION OF POLICY AT THE LONDON
    CONFERENCE 163

APPENDIX E

REPORT OF THE MONETARY AND FINANCIAL COMMIS-
SION OF THE LONDON CONFERENCE 167

APPENDIX F

BRITISH IMPERIAL DECLARATION ON MONETARY
    POLICY 179

APPENDIX G

PRESIDENT ROOSEVELT'S RADIO ADDRESS OF OCTOBER
    22, 1933 183
INDEX 191

INTRODUCTION

Economic and political discussions and controversies of the year 1933 have centered in large measure around monetary issues in relation to economic recovery. When the year began the world had already passed through 18 months of growing disorganization in the sphere of foreign exchanges, but there was hope that just ahead lay the possibility of an international agreement which would restore order and stability. An attempt to reach such an agreement was made at the first session of the World Monetary and Economic Conference, held in London in June and July, after months of preparation and preliminary consultations among the governments mainly concerned. That attempt failed, and monetary instability and uncertainty, which had increased greatly during the first half of the year, continued unabated into the second. The world is today confronted for the second time since the ending of the World War with the necessity of making a vital choice in the domain of its basic monetary organization.

Prior to 1914 there existed an international monetary system which was almost universal in the scope of its functioning. The international character of the system resulted from the fact that in all the important countries gold was the common standard of value. Under this international monetary standard the foreign exchanges were stable within narrow and defined limits. The operation of the exchanges underwent marked change with the widespread abandonment of the gold standard during the war. For some years after the cessation of hostilities, national currencies were subject to wide and frequent fluctuations in terms of each other—a condition which existed until the principal nations of the world decided to restore the gold standard and, one after another, carried this decision into effect. Stable foreign exchanges then prevailed until the middle of 1931 when, as a result of the current economic depression, the international monetary system again broke down.

The question whether the international gold standard should once more be restored is much more difficult and complicated today than it was in the years immediately following the war. When the international financial conferences at Brussels and Genoa grappled, in 1920 and 1922, with the problem of disrupted monetary systems and fluctuating foreign exchanges, there was a general recognition of the fact that the breakdown of the international monetary system based on the gold standard was one of the unfortunate consequences of the world conflict. It was taken for granted by responsible statesmen in all important countries that a restoration of such a system was necessary and desirable. Both conferences pronounced emphatically in favor of the re-establishment of an international gold standard and agreed upon the conditions which had to be fulfilled for this purpose.

Since the second breakdown of the international gold standard, however, the view has become widespread in many countries that that standard has become inherently defective. Accordingly, it is held that an alternative system must be devised. Proposals for a substitute monetary organization have run in terms of managed currency systems, with the primary emphasis upon the control of price levels rather than upon the maintenance of foreign exchange stability. This alternative assumed importance as a practical monetary issue when the British government, following the abandonment of the gold standard in September 1931, began to lend some measure of support to the managed currency idea. The issue became still more sharply defined after the United States departed from the gold standard in the spring of 1933, and especially when the gold purchase plan of price regulation was introduced.

While in recent months the monetary problem has loomed large in the public eye and has attracted widespread interest and attention, the complex underlying issues involved have not been clearly defined. The main purpose of this brief study is to set forth and analyze the monetary issues that now agitate the world, as well as the conflicts of ideas and policies which have so far prevented any effective solution.

These issues have found expression during the current year mainly in connection with international discussions and negotiations. It was on such occasions as the meeting of the Preparatory Commission of Experts for the World Monetary and Economic Conference held at Geneva in January, the consultations between President Roosevelt and the representatives of the principal foreign governments which took place at Washington in April and May, and the London sessions of the World Conference itself in June and July, that the national differences of views and policies were brought to a focus and were made the subject of prolonged discussions.

These discussions covered all of the underlying basic monetary issues of our day, and an analysis of what took place at Geneva, at Washington, and at London provides an extremely convenient vehicle for a presentation of the issues involved. Hence the major portion of the text is devoted to such an analysis. In the concluding chapters the monetary position of the world in general since the London Conference is surveyed and an analysis is made of recent developments in the United States, including the gold purchase plan.

CHAPTER I

BREAKDOWN OF THE GOLD STANDARD

The World War brought about a complete disruption of monetary stability everywhere. At the end of the conflict, all the countries of the world were off the gold standard, either through suspension of redemption or through embargoes on gold exports, and the foreign exchange rates fluctuated widely in spite of attempts made by many countries to minimize these oscillations by means of control devices. For a period of several years after the war, the United States was the only country that had returned to the full gold standard.

While the Brussels and Genoa conferences of 1920 and 1922 had definitely expressed the view that a return to the gold standard was indispensable to economic reconstruction, it was not until the complete monetary collapse of Central Europe in 1922 and 1923 that the leading countries decided to co-operate in the re-establishment of the gold standard at the earliest possible moment. Between 1923 and 1929, in part as a result of international co-operation, as in the case of Austria, Hungary, and Germany, and in part as a result of independent action, virtually the whole world returned to a gold standard either formally or *de facto*. The only notable exceptions were China and Persia, which were on the silver standard, and Brazil, Spain, Turkey, and several smaller countries, which were still operating on the basis of inconvertible paper. Foreign exchange stability was in this manner restored and control measures were generally abandoned.

A second breakdown of the gold standard occurred

after the economic depression was well under way. During the first two years of the depression there were but a few isolated defections from the gold standard. Three countries abandoned gold in December 1929 and one in July 1931. It was not until after September 1931 that the wholesale breakdown of the international monetary system began. Great Britain suspended the redemption of her currency on September 21, 1931. Fifteen other countries abandoned gold in the last four months of that year, and another nine followed suit in 1932. The measures of foreign exchange control which began to be reintroduced during the early stages of the depression also spread rapidly after Great Britain's departure from gold.

The degree of depreciation of the currencies which are no longer linked with gold has not, during the present monetary dislocation, been comparable to that in the early post-war years when many currencies went almost to zero. However, in most cases the depreciation has been substantial, as may be seen from the frontispiece chart. By the beginning of 1933 the Japanese yen had dropped to only 42 per cent of its gold parity, and the pound sterling was worth only 69 per cent of its former value.

These substantial alterations in the currency values of two very important commercial countries, accompanied as they were—in the case of these, as well as of all other depreciated currencies—by wide fluctuations, exercised a disorganizing effect on international trade and financial relations. Dislocation in this vital sphere of economic activity was increased by the existence of a large accumulation and variety of foreign exchange control measures which had far-reaching repercussions on the volume and direction of commodity trade, as well as on movements of capital and the whole organization of credit.

I. MONETARY POSITION OF THE WORLD AT THE BEGINNING OF 1933

The table on page 8 shows the currency standard position of 50 countries on January 1, 1933. It will be noted that of this list, which includes all the important commercial nations of the world, 30 countries were officially off the gold standard. Of these, 14 had introduced foreign exchange control, while most of the other 16 were exercising some measure of unofficial regulation of their exchange rates. Nine countries were still nominally on the gold standard and were attempting to maintain their gold parities by means of official control measures of varying degrees of stringency and with a decidedly uneven degree of success. In the case of some of them—for example, Germany and Czechoslovakia —official parities prevailed. In the case of others—notably Austria, Hungary, Yugoslavia, Rumania—the measures of control were only partly effective and the currency units were in fact depreciated. Only eleven countries remained on the full gold standard, and even some of these were imposing certain limitations on a free operation of that standard.

The four categories into which the nations listed in the table on page 8 are classified require a brief explanation. A country is on a full gold standard when it fulfills, through legal requirement or in practice, the following four fundamental conditions:

1. Its basic monetary unit—the dollar in the United States, the pound sterling in Great Britain, the franc in France, etc.—must be defined in terms of a fixed quantity of gold of a specified fineness.

2. It must either make provision for an unlimited coinage of gold or else lay an obligation upon some specially designated agency to purchase, at a fixed rate, all gold brought to it.

3. All means of payment within a country must be freely redeemable on demand at a fixed rate in gold, or

MONETARY STANDARD POSITION OF 50 COUNTRIES, JANUARY 1, 1933

Off the Gold Standard and with Depreciated Currencies		Nominally on the Gold Standard with Old Parities Maintained through Official Control	On Full Gold Standard[d]
Without Official Control	With Official Control		
Australia	Argentine	Austria	Albania
British India	Bolivia	Bulgaria	Belgium
British Malaya	Brazil[a]	Czechoslovakia	Dantzig
Canada	Chile	Estonia	Dutch East
Egypt	Colombia	Germany	Indies
Finland	Denmark	Hungary	France
Great Britain	Ecuador	Latvia	Italy
Irish Free State	Greece	Rumania	Lithuania
Mexico	Japan	Yugoslavia	The Netherlands
New Zealand[b]	Persia[c]		Poland
Norway	Portugal		Switzerland
Palestine	Spain[a]		The United
Peru	Turkey[a]		States
Siam	Uruguay[b]		
Sweden			
Union of South Africa			

[a] The gold standard was never officially resumed after the World War.

[b] The gold standard was never officially re-established after the war, but there was a *de facto* return to pre-war gold parities.

[c] Persia had a silver standard until March 1932, when a gold parity was legally adopted, although the exchange rate followed the pound sterling.

[d] See p. 7.

in claims to gold located abroad. This must be true at least for purposes of international transactions.

4. There must be complete freedom of gold exports and imports.

The fulfillment of these four conditions provides an effective and convenient mechanism for maintaining the relative values of the various national currency units in a state of stability. The fact that the national monetary units are defined in terms of fixed quantities of gold makes it possible to compare any two of them and to establish a parity between them. The fact that under the gold standard there exists in each country adhering to it an unlimited market for gold at a fixed price (through coinage or purchase by the Treasury or the bank of issue); that gold can, generally speaking, always be obtained at a fixed price in exchange for all forms of national currency; and that gold can always be freely shipped from one country to another, assures that deviations from the gold parities would be confined within narrow limits.

These limits are, in fact, determined by the costs involved in shipping gold from one country to another. Whenever, for example, the price of a bill of exchange expressed in dollars rises, in terms of the pound sterling, above the cost of shipping an equivalent amount of metallic gold across the Atlantic plus the loss of interest during the time of shipment, the "gold import point" of the dollar would be reached, and gold would move from Great Britain to the United States. In the reverse case, the "gold export point" would be reached, and the movement of gold would be in the opposite direction.

These "gold points," while somewhat different for each pair of countries (depending on the distance between them, the transportation facilities, etc.), are always so close together and are so easily determined that, under the gold standard, the values of national currency units in terms of each other vary but slightly. For example, when both the dollar and the pound sterling were exchangeable for gold, the amount of pure gold contained in the pound was 4.866 times that contained in the dollar. A pound was, therefore, worth at par of exchange, $4.866. For several continuous decades before the war the value of the pound never rose above $4.91 and never dropped below $4.82.

In this manner an international monetary system comes into existence—not through the substitution of a single world system of currency and credit for the separate national monetary systems, but rather through the existence of facilities for co-ordinating these national systems into an international complex. The basis of such co-ordination is a standard of value, common to all the component monetary systems and operating through the mechanism of stable foreign exchange rates.

Failure to fulfill any of the four basic conditions enumerated above would constitute an abandonment of the gold standard. In practice, such abandonment usually involves the last two of these conditions, either singly or together. When gold ceases to be freely available for foreign shipment, the limits, beyond which the foreign exchange value of the currency units affected cannot fluctuate, no longer exist. Such currency units usually become subject to wide and frequent fluctuations in terms of other currency units, although these fluctuations may, at least for a time, be confined within comparatively narrow limits by means of a large variety of measures of control.

Some countries introduce control measures for the purpose of enabling them to remain nominally on the gold standard. This means that officially the currency of such a country still remains exchangeable for gold, at the legal rate, but that redemption is not made freely on demand. The bank of issue is given the right to refuse redemption whenever the currency position is considered to be in danger. In order to prevent the foreign exchange value of the currency unit from depreciating under these conditions, an agency, specially designated for the purpose, is given control over all transactions involving foreign currencies.

Such control is successful if the system is sufficiently stringent to prevent violations of the regulatory measures. When substantial violations occur, a country has, in practice, two rates of foreign exchange: an official, and therefore stable, rate, which governs transactions over which the control measures are effective; and an unofficial, and usually depreciated and fluctuating rate, which prevails in transactions that escape control.

Countries which are officially off the gold standard typically do not endeavor to control the exchange rates of their currency units. They allow these rates to fluctuate, but very often take measures to prevent the fluctuations from attaining too large an amplitude. For this purpose two principal methods of procedure are open to them. They can introduce official control over all foreign exchange transactions, as the countries which remain nominally on the gold standard do, but apply such control to smoothing out short-term fluctuations, rather than to maintaining a definite party. Or, for the purpose of accomplishing the same result without subjecting foreign exchange transactions to any official control, their authorities can intervene unofficially from time to time in the foreign exchange market by buying and selling foreign exchange.[1] An outstanding example of this sort of intervention is found in the operation of the British Exchange Equalization Account.

In the case of countries which introduce official con-

[1] Intervention of this sort is also often exercised by the authorities of countries which are still on the full gold standard, in cases of exceptional temporary difficulties.

trol, the success of measures of this sort depends upon the effectiveness of administering the regulatory prescriptions. In the case of countries which employ the method of unofficial intervention, success or failure clearly depends upon whether or not they possess the necessary resources, in the form of gold or foreign currencies, with which to operate in the foreign exchange market.

The abandonment of the gold standard by at least some of the commercially important nations or a widespread introduction of foreign exchange control measures means the breaking down of an international monetary system into a series of more or less isolated national systems. Such dissociation has far-reaching economic consequences. The principal advantage of stable foreign exchanges is that they facilitate commercial and financial intercourse among nations by providing an international standard of value. It is universally recognized that foreign exchange stability maintained by means of control measures cannot take the place of a free operation of the gold standard. It can be effective only if trade and financial transactions are subjected to regulation, and this inevitably curtails trade, obstructs the payment of debts, and disrupts credit relations in general. Whatever other ends such control measures may serve, the type of foreign exchange stability which they provide seldom fails, in the final analysis, to disorganize international trade and financial relations, which stable exchanges are fundamentally designed to facilitate and subserve. They are not, therefore, regarded as a feasible permanent alternative to the gold standard.[2]

[2] For a detailed discussion of the various existing systems of foreign exchange control and their economic effects, the reader is referred to the forthcoming Brookings Institution publication in this series, entitled, *Foreign Exchange Control: Techniques and Effects.*

II. OUTLOOK FOR RESTORATION OF THE GOLD STANDARD

The outlook at the beginning of 1933 for a restoration of an international monetary system based on gold was much more hopeful than the long list of departures from the gold standard might indicate. After all, decision as to the character of the world's monetary organization rests primarily with the principal trading nations, the less important countries being, in practice, compelled to follow. And in January 1933, of the ten largest foreign trade nations of the world,[3] only four—Great Britain, Canada, Japan, and India—possessed currencies no longer linked to gold. Five of the others—the United States, France, The Netherlands, Belgium, and Italy —had maintained their currencies at par by a free operation of the gold standard, while the sixth, Germany, had escaped depreciation by means of control measures and stood ready to return to a full gold standard whenever general conditions would permit. Moreover, a number of the nations in the non-gold column—the British Dominions and the Scandinavian countries— which had abandoned the gold standard together with Great Britain, were making more or less successful attempts to keep the exchange rates of their currencies moving in unison with the pound sterling, thus maintaining over a large trading area a temporary condition approximating foreign exchange stability, and thereby emphasizing their basic belief in the desirability of such stability in the interests of international trade and financial relations.

As a practical proposition, the question of a universal return to stable foreign exchanges through a restoration

[3] The United States, Great Britain, Germany, France, Canada, The Netherlands, Belgium, Japan, Italy, and India.

of an international gold standard was a matter of decision by Great Britain and Japan—and, in the final analysis, principally by the former—to link their currencies once more to gold, either at the old parity or at some new value. In the making of this decision, the emerging advocacy of a managed-paper system as a substitute for an international gold standard was not a real obstacle to a restoration of that standard. For, as we shall see in the next chapter, the official British support of the managed currency system was never more than half-hearted, the British government being primarily concerned with the establishment of economic conditions which, in its view, were indispensable to the functioning of an international economic organization and an international monetary system.

In this general form, the monetary problem was the subject of much discussion through the year 1932. It was one of the principal topics on the agenda of the Lausanne Conference, held in June and July of that year. That important parley—after disposing of the reparation question, a solution of which was its immediate objective—decided that further consultation and action were needed for the purpose of devising "the measures necessary to solve the other economic and financial difficulties which are responsible for or may prolong the present world crisis." In order to accomplish this, the statesmen gathered at Lausanne resolved to convoke a World Monetary and Economic Conference, and, in enumerating the questions which, in their judgment, demanded examination, they laid special emphasis on "the necessity of restoring the currencies on a healthy basis."

While the Lausanne resolution was expressed in vague and general terms, the connotation of this last phrase was not left in any doubt. The restoration of currencies was urged for the purpose of "making it possible to abolish measures of exchange control and to remove transfer difficulties." Furthermore, the participants in the Lausanne Conference announced themselves "impressed with the vital need of facilitating the revival of international trade." Clearly, none of these objectives could be attained in the absence of an international monetary standard, and one of the chief reasons for convoking the World Conference was to provide an opportunity for agreement between the gold and the non-gold countries on the character of such a standard and the conditions for its re-establishment.

CHAPTER II

GENEVA: ADJUSTMENT OF CONFLICTING VIEWS

The responsibility for preparing and eventually convoking the World Monetary and Economic Conference was assigned to the League of Nations. As the first step, the League created a Preparatory Commission of Experts to draw up a program for the future parley, to subject the questions to be discussed to a preliminary examination, and to make recommendations for the guidance of the conference itself. The commission began its work at a session lasting from October 31 to November 9, 1932, and completed its task at a second session, January 9-19, 1933. Both meetings took place at Geneva. Eighteen countries, including all the commercially important nations, were represented, either directly by appointment of their respective governments, or indirectly by invitation of the League Council.[1]

In its monetary work, the commission surveyed the whole field of outstanding currency and credit problems with a view, first, to clarifying the divergences of national views and policies, and second, to discovering ways of reconciling the existing conflicts and thus removing the obstacles which stood in the way of agreement. Apart from the fundamental issue of the gold standard, the commission's discussion was rendered extremely difficult by the existence of a sharp divergence of opinion with

[1] Three Americans were members of the commission: Dr. E. E. Day of the Rockefeller Foundation, and Professor J. H. Williams of Harvard University, as appointees of the United States government, and Mr. Leon Fraser, president of the Bank for International Settlements, as a representative of that important institution.

reference to the question whether a rise in commodity prices was a necessary preliminary to the re-establishment of exchange stability and the restoration of the gold standard, and whether, if so, such a rise in prices could and should be brought about by concerted monetary action. In the end the commission succeeded in reaching what appeared to be a fairly acceptable compromise as to general principles and procedures. This compromise was embodied in the commission's final report, known as the Annotated Agenda, which constitutes the experts' recommendations on the subject of general economic recovery and the role of the monetary problem in the recovery process.

I. THE GOLD STANDARD ISSUE

Three distinct points of view were reflected in the discussions of the Commission of Experts concerning the desirability and the possibility of return to an international gold standard system. At one extreme is the opinion that the gold standard has outlived its usefulness—if, indeed, it ever did provide a satisfactory monetary mechanism—and that the time has come to substitute for it what the advocates of this view consider a more scientific monetary organization, operating on the basis of a standard of value which would be expressed in terms of a managed-paper currency related to a chosen price index. At the other extreme is the view that, in the existing state of scientific economic knowledge and general economic and social organization, the gold standard can be the only satisfactory basis for an efficient monetary system and that unless it is restored the world is doomed to economic retrogression. Between these two is a third view, in accordance with which both systems are equally feasible, with the theoretical advantage in favor of managed-paper rather than gold, but with the practical advantage the other way round. Since, in the opinion of the advocates of this view, the gold standard has broken down mainly because of the inability or the unwillingness of the nations of the world to fulfill certain economic conditions indispensable to its proper functioning, its re-establishment would be fruitless unless it was clear that these conditions could and would be fulfilled. If this should prove not to be the case, then a managed-paper standard is to be preferred to a restoration of the gold standard.

A. Arguments for a Permanent Abandonment of Gold

The principal argument in favor of a deliberate and permanent abandonment of the gold standard as a basis for an international monetary system is that such a standard fails to provide for a stable commodity price level. Stability of this sort, it is urged, can be achieved only by linking the currency unit to a price index, rather than to a single commodity like gold, and by managing currency and credit with a view to preventing substantial fluctuations in this index.

This argument implies, first, that a stability of commodity prices can be secured by means of monetary action or management, mainly in the form of a manipulation of the volume of currency and credit; and, second, that the maintenance of such stability would confer great benefits upon economic and social organization, even though it might render the attainment of foreign exchange stability difficult, if not altogether impossible.

The term "price stability" refers not to individual

prices but to the general level of prices. Such a price level is an index number of the individual prices of a large number of commodities, selected for their importance in economic life and weighted in accordance with their relative importance. The result is an indicator of a general average trend of prices, rather than of the separate price movements of individual commodities, which, in a normal economic situation, undergo constant changes with respect to one another. The "purchasing power of money" is then defined as the inverse of this price level: it increases when the price level falls, and decreases when the price level rises.

The main advantages attributed to a stable price level and, consequently, to a constant purchasing power of money, are twofold: First, debtor-creditor relationships would become more equitable; and second, economic activity in general would no longer be subject to the fluctuations involved in the so-called business cycle.

The emphasis in such a system would necessarily be on monetary management in relation to domestic, rather than international, factors, since each nation, by its own authority, can manipulate only its own currency and credit and, therefore, manage only its own price level. Foreign exchange rates would either be left to fluctuate, or else be also manipulated as one of the instruments for maintaining a stable domestic price level. Alternatively, the theory envisages the possibility of international price management, through concerted action by national authorities, which, it is expected, would give each national currency unit constant domestic purchasing power and, therefore, stable relative value in terms of other currency units.

The advocates of the managed-paper system are fully

aware of the fact that a general acceptance of the policies involved in the establishment of such a system must, under existing conditions, lead to the creation of a series of independent national monetary systems. This, because the co-ordination of such systems into an international complex would require one of two things: either the setting up of an international authority to regulate currency and credit in all countries, or else far-reaching agreement among nations to act only in accordance with their common decisions. It is clear that neither of these arrangements is practicable in the existing political state of the world. Therefore, national attempts to maintain stable domestic price levels might, it is recognized, lead to a disruption of international trade and financial relations and force the world into a permanent organization based, more or less, on national economic isolation.

Some of the prominent advocates of managed-paper currency do not, however, regard this as a necessarily disastrous development. They argue that while an international monetary system has the advantage of facilitating international economic intercourse, and thus of conferring upon humanity whatever benefits accrue from an international division of labor and a more efficient distribution of nationally localized natural resources, it has the vital disadvantage of rendering the national economy of each country subject to foreign influences, especially in the monetary field, over which the people and the authorities of that country have little or no control. They regard the uncertainties thus resulting from an international system as far outweighing its benefits, and argue that national monetary—and, consequently, economic—organization is, on balance, preferable, at least until a system of international monetary management can be created. The argument for managed-paper currency is thus, in practice, inextricably bound up with the movement for economic nationalism.[2]

B. Arguments for Restoration of the Gold Standard

The argument in favor of the gold standard and, therefore, against the managed-currency system, rests on a number of basic disagreements with the postulates of the view we have just described. In the first place, many advocates of a return to gold believe that proponents of managed currency exaggerate the importance of the monetary factor in the determination of the price level. In their view, the process of price formation is a much more complicated one, involving many non-monetary factors which cannot be regulated by monetary action. They are convinced, therefore, that a stable price level cannot be achieved merely by a manipulation of currency and credit.

In the second place, they doubt whether the advantages claimed for a stable price level would, in reality, confer any far-reaching benefits on economic and social organization. They maintain that the price structure is much too complex to find adequate expression in so generalized a concept as a price level, and that the movements of individual commodity prices or of groups of prices are much too important not to have determining effects on general business conditions and on debtor-creditor relations.

[2] The discussion in this chapter is entirely in terms of managed-paper currency. The proposal for currency management by alteration of the gold content of the monetary unit, of which the "compensated dollar" plan is an outstanding example, was not even reflected in the Geneva discussions. It came into prominence some months later. See Chaps. V-VI.

Finally, the advocates of a return to the gold stand-ard regard the disruption of the international monetary system and its attendant international economic organiza-tion as a disastrous price to pay for the benefits which are claimed for economic nationalism and which they consider highly problematical. They argue that in the past humanity has achieved its greatest economic de-velopment on the basis of a substantial measure of inter-national trade and financial intercourse, and that to dis-rupt such intercourse permanently or to reduce it to com-paratively small proportions would lead to a prolonged and profound economic dislocation everywhere and promise, in the end, at best nothing more tangible than a leap into the unknown.

The advocates of gold admit readily that violent al-terations in commodity prices are highly injurious in their effects, and that efforts should be made to prevent their occurrence. But they argue that such preventive action involves much more than the mere machinery of currency and credit and can be successful only if rooted in general economic as well as monetary policies. And for purposes of such action, the maintenance of an inter-national gold standard offers advantages, rather than obstacles.[3]

C. The Geneva Line-Up

At Geneva the view that the restoration of an inter-national gold standard is essential if a period of mone-tary chaos and economic retrogression is to be avoided was urged primarily by commission members from the United States, France, Italy, and Holland. Outright op-position to the gold standard was not officially sponsored

[3] For an exhaustive discussion of this subject see the *Final Report of the Gold Delegation of the League of Nations,* 1932.

by any of the experts. However, the establishment of a managed-paper currency system was advanced, mainly by the British experts, as a feasible substitute for the gold standard and one which should be adopted unless the conditions indispensable to a proper functioning of the gold standard could be fulfilled. Arguments of this nature were evidently regarded as useful in procuring the necessary modification of those economic policies which, it was held, had been impeding the successful operation of the gold standard in the past and had led to a breakdown of the international gold standard system.

As a matter of fact, all the spokesmen for the important countries were in agreement on the practical desirability, if not on the relative theoretical merits, of an international gold standard. The principal British representative himself referred to it as "a wonderful instrument which has served the world in the past exceedingly well and has largely contributed to the development of our present high standard of life and civilization." He also described his country as having "great interest in international trade," and being, accordingly, "as anxious as any other country to see an efficient international monetary system re-established." But he laid down a number of fundamental conditions which, in his opinion, must be fulfilled before his country would decide to return to gold; and it was on some of these, and especially on their application, that the experts really disagreed.

There were three fundamental conditions laid down by Great Britain and the other non-gold countries. They were as follows:

1. The gap between the level of costs of production and that of commodity prices, produced by the recent

drastic fall in prices, must be closed by a rise in the latter.

2. An international economic balance must be re-established through a satisfactory settlement of the war-debt controversy, a removal of foreign exchange controls, and a substantial modification of economic policies to be achieved by an abandonment of extraordinary trade restrictions and a progressive lowering, as well as eventual relative stabilization, of customs tariffs.

3. Agreement must be reached on a number of technical reforms of the gold standard system, such as a reduction in the percentage of reserves, the abolition of gold coins, and the establishment of a system of central banking collaboration.

Unless these conditions were fulfilled, it was stated, the non-gold countries would be content to follow their then current policies of operating on the basis of national systems of paper currencies, continuing, at the same time, their effort to co-ordinate these systems, under the leadership of Great Britain, mainly with a view toward trade co-operation within their area. They were represented as determined to pursue this course of action, rather than to join in any efforts to re-establish the gold standard under what they regarded as unworkable conditions, and thus expose themselves to the dangers of another breakdown of that standard with all its attendant dislocations and evils.

More specifically on the question of the stabilization of their currencies in terms of foreign exchanges, the experts from these countries argued that it was impossible for their governments to commit themselves to any fixed rates until they knew what the general course of events would be. Especially, they urged, was this true of price movements. For example, if gold prices—that is, prices in countries still on the gold standard—rose, then the establishment of equilibrium between costs and prices in the non-gold countries would be possible on the basis of a higher gold content of their currency units than would be the case if gold prices continued to fall.

The commission members from the gold countries were in general agreement with their colleagues that an adjustment of prices and costs is a necessary condition for the restoration and future maintenance of the gold standard. Some of them expressed the view, however, that a rise in prices alone, without at least a certain amount of reduction of costs, would not be the most desirable method of effecting such an adjustment. They were also in general agreement on the need for a technical reform of the gold standard system and on the necessity for the fulfillment of the conditions enumerated under (2) above. But they argued that the fulfillment of most of these conditions would be impossible unless it were undertaken concurrently with the decision to return to a stability of foreign exchanges, and, therefore, to an international gold standard. They pointed out that fluctuating foreign exchanges represent an immense potential risk of sudden alterations in the terms of trade among countries, and that unless this risk were removed no country could consent to forego the use of trade restrictions which provide a weapon for combating these changes. The fulfillment of the conditions laid down would have for its principal objective the cessation of economic warfare and the promotion of an economic equilibrium, whereas in the absence of stable foreign exchanges, such warfare would be merely intensified and the already existing disequilibrium rendered more widespread and profound.

While agreeing that the choice of new currency unit values would be an important element in establishing an equilibrium between costs and prices, they argued that such a choice cannot, under any circumstances, be made with any degree of precision. Whatever the value chosen, the interests of some groups would be temporarily promoted, while those of other groups would be sacrificed. For example, a relatively low level of stabilization would, in general, favor the debtors and the business interests, and would be prejudicial to the creditors and the financial interests. But since all these interests are interrelated and are not clearly defined, a nice balance between them, which would be the basis of an ideal currency unit value, is impossible to attain.

In the meantime, unstabilized exchanges, operating inevitably as an instrument of economic warfare, would continue to play havoc with almost every phase of economic activity and thus affect adversely every element in the community. The disadvantages of continued economic disorganization, resulting from too great delay in effecting the stabilization of foreign exchanges, they held, would more than offset any possible advantages to be derived from what, in any event, must necessarily be a merely approximate balancing of the interests involved in the choice of new parities.

II. DISAGREEMENT ON ROLE OF COMMODITY PRICES

The difficult problem of commodity prices, in its relation to monetary restoration and economic recovery in general, was the second and the really outstanding major issue before the financial experts of the Preparatory Commission. On this question, two distinct views were reflected in the Geneva discussions. One was that a sub-

stantial rise in commodity prices is an indispensable preliminary and conditioning factor in economic recovery
and that it must occur before the world's currencies can
be re-established on an internationally stable basis. The
other was that rising prices are an indication of, rather
than a preliminary condition to, economic recovery, and
that neither can be brought about without foreign exchange stability.

A. Price Recovery as an Antecedent to Economic Recovery

The view that price recovery must precede economic
recovery was urged by the experts of Great Britain and
the other non-gold countries. They pointed out that the
only possible alternative to a rise in commodity prices
would be a further reduction of costs, mainly through a
scaling down of wages, salaries, and debt charges. They
felt that while by this method the world might, conceiva-
bly, in time work itself out of the present depression, the
adoption of this course of action would mean, for the
time being, a further intensification of the depression,
mined effort to raise prices, accompanied by the reduction
with all its attendant dislocation and suffering. A deter-
of one element of costs—namely, interest rates—was advocated by these experts as a distinctly preferable course
of action.

The lowering of interest rates was, indeed, put forward as an important instrument for raising commodity
prices. Credit would thus become cheap. It should also be
made plentiful by means of appropriate action on the
part of central banking authorities, through open market
operations and in other ways. Cheap and plentiful credit
would stimulate business enterprise and thus bring about

a rise in prices. A further stimulation should be given by programs of public works. In short, a policy which has become familiarly known in recent years under the name of "reflation," should be vigorously pursued.

Emphasis was, however, laid on the fact that what was really necessary was not a rise in isolated national price levels, but a rise in gold prices, which would inaugurate a general upward trend and pave the way for a restoration of the gold standard. This meant in effect that promotion of a price rise should be undertaken mainly by the countries still on the gold standard. A process of "reflation" in such countries, accompanied by a resumption of international movements of capital, would bring about a redistribution of gold reserves and open the way for a similar development in other countries.

At the same time, the fulfillment of the second of the three sets of conditions outlined on pages 23-24 was urged as a concurrent and powerful instrument in inducing a rise in commodity prices. In other words, a substantial modification of policies relating to international trade barriers, foreign exchange controls, and the war debts, would be indispensable to the price-raising process.

B. Price Recovery as an Accompaniment of Economic Recovery

The experts of the gold standard countries were united on the proposition that the rise in prices which was advocated could be brought about only as an accompaniment of general economic recovery. With reference to the question whether in the process of establishing equilibrium between cost and prices the principal emphasis should be placed on adjustment of the latter rather than the former, there was difference of opinion. But there was general agreement that both elements would probably have to come into operation before genuine recovery could be assured.

Economic recovery, they argued, means fundamentally an increase in demand for goods and services, national and international, and a consequent expansion of production and trade. A proper functioning of a credit organization, again nationally and internationally, is a vital factor in this process. And whatever might be accomplished within a given country, internationally there can be no hope of a resumption of credit relations until an international standard of value exists once more. Without such a standard, independent movements of national price levels under the impetus of unco-ordinated domestic price-raising measures would merely serve to increase the already existing maladjustments in the world price structure and thus retard rather than promote general economic recovery through a curtailment of international trade.

Moreover, they maintained that efforts on the part of important commercial nations to seek foreign trade advantage through currency depreciation inevitably lead to a fall in gold prices. They pointed to the experience of the countries which were still on the gold standard and which found themselves compelled to meet the competition of the non-gold countries by reducing the prices of their exports.

So far as the relation of a rise in prices to the stabilization of the non-gold currencies was concerned, therefore, the British argument that a rise in prices should precede stabilization was, in their opinion, of the vicious-circle type. This opinion was based upon their conviction that gold prices cannot really rise until there is a general expansion of economic activity, while some of the vital obstacles to such an expansion cannot be removed until foreign exchanges are stabilized.[4]

III. EXPERTS' RECOMMENDATIONS

Confronted with these differences of opinion, the Commission of Experts could not, in many of its final recommendations, escape vagueness and inconclusiveness. On some of the fundamental issues, the Annotated Agenda recorded no agreement. Nevertheless, the general outlines of the program which the experts proposed to the governments of the world stand out with adequate clarity.

On the question of the future monetary standard, after surveying the arguments for and against national and international organization, gold and managed-paper standard, as well as the possibilities for the introduction of silver into the monetary systems—a question placed on the agenda at the insistence of the United States—they agreed to recommend the re-establishment of an international gold standard, free from the restraints of foreign exchange control, with very little admixture of price management, and without any dilution of gold with silver. In their Annotated Agenda they said:

The restoration of a satisfactory international monetary standard is clearly of primary importance. The World Conference, in the absence of another international standard likely to be universally acceptable, will have to consider how the conditions for a successful restoration of a free gold standard could be fulfilled. In our view, among the essential conditions are the restoration of equilibrium between prices and costs and, in the future, such a reasonable degree of stability of prices as the world measure of

---

[4] This summary of the Geneva debates is based on the official résumés of proceedings and the author's conversations in Geneva.

value should properly possess. . . . As the only international monetary standard which is at present likely to command universal acceptance is the gold standard, the idea of introducing bimetallism must be regarded as impracticable. . . . On the assumption that no form of bimetallism will prove acceptable, silver is unsuitable for extensive inclusion in the metallic reserves of a central bank.

In making these recommendations, the Commission of Experts reiterated the conclusions that had been set forth in two important international documents issued in 1932. These were the Majority Report of the Gold Delegation of the League of Nations (May 1932) and the Resolution of the Board of Directors of the Bank for International Settlements (July 1932). Further on in their recommendations, the Geneva experts followed very closely the proposals contained in the two earlier documents as to the conditions necessary for restoring the gold standard and for ensuring its proper functioning in the future. These conditions, apart from the technical measures designed to improve the functioning of the gold standard, may be summarized as follows:

The restoration of the gold standard must, of necessity, be a relatively long process, proceeding in stages. However, for the immediate purpose of economic recovery, only a decision to inaugurate this process is essential. This decision must be accompanied by willingness on the part of the principal nations concerned to take a number of important measures, nationally, as well as internationally.

The principal national measures proposed were in the field of public finance, the experts recommending that (1) "revenue and expenditure, not only of the state budget proper, but also of the budgets of public enterprise (railways, etc.) and of local authorities should be balanced"; and (2) "it will be necessary to create and maintain healthy conditions in the internal money and capital market and at all costs to avoid an inflationary increase of the note circulation in order to meet government deficits."

The general proposals for international action related to (1) "the solution of major outstanding political problems," as a contribution to a restoration of confidence; (2) a satisfactory settlement of inter-governmental debts; (3) "a return to a reasonable degree of freedom in the movement of goods and services"; and (4) "a return to a freedom in the foreign exchange markets and in the movement of capital."

With respect to the return to freer international trade, the experts stressed the necessity of progressive and substantial mitigation of the existing trade barriers. With respect to the abolition of foreign exchange controls, they emphasized the probable need of adjusting private international obligations, especially on the short-term account. The principal object of all these measures would be to permit an expansion of economic activity and to open the way to a rise in commodity prices.

On the special question of prices, the commission expressed its general opinion that "some increase in the level of world prices is highly desirable and would be the first sign of world recovery." After pointing out that easy money conditions already exist in all the important countries, they recommended the continuation and development of a liberal credit policy "designed to promote a healthy expansion of business." They expressed no opinion on the possible efficacy of public works programs as instruments of price-raising, except to serve warning that such a policy would be detrimental, rather than beneficial, unless the programs were "financed by borrowings from the market," the policy itself "kept within reasonable limits," and the whole development did not "result in deteriorating government credit." But they were emphatic in urging the view that the real basis of a rise in prices must be an increase in the general demand for commodities, and that such increased demand should be expected mainly "as an outcome of increasing confidence in the general financial and economic structure." They concluded their price discussion as follows:

If it is found that political and monetary authorities are endeavoring to carry out a policy which holds out some hope of ultimate improvement, we believe that the public will soon respond by resuming normal economic developments. We venture to suggest that a general adoption of the policy outlined in this report—aiming at the restoration of currencies on a healthy basis, financial reconstruction, a greater freedom in the movement of goods, and some immediate measures to give evidence of its practical application—would be a decisive step towards this revival of confidence.

With respect to the stabilization of foreign exchanges the experts could not agree on any specific formula, although their advocacy of such stabilization was clearly implicit in their general recommendation in favor of a return to the gold standard and in their whole discussion of recovery measures. They stated that "the time when it will be possible for a particular country to return to the gold standard and the exchange parity at which such a return can safely be made will necessarily depend on the conditions in that country as well as those abroad, and these questions can only be determined by the proper authorities in each country separately." They sought, however, to strengthen this statement somewhat by contending that "in practice, certain countries are in a key position in that the re-establishment of a free gold standard by them would influence action in a number of other countries." This was clearly an invitation to Great Britain to take the lead.

In addition they recommended that "efforts should be made to avoid a competition between states to acquire a temporary advantage in international trade by depreciating the external value of their currency below such a point as is required to re-establish internal equilibrium." Moreover, it was urged that, pending the final determination of the new values of depreciated currencies, "it is advisable for the authorities regulating the currencies concerned to smooth out, so far as their resources permit, day-to-day fluctuations in the exchanges due to speculative influences, by buying and selling foreign currencies." In this manner, it was felt, violent fluctuations in the exchange rates would be avoided during the transition from unstable to stable foreign exchanges.

These were the issues surveyed by the Geneva experts and the principal recommendations in the monetary sphere which they made to the governments of the world. In the program of recovery upon which they finally agreed, the central place was assigned to a re-establishment of an international economic system which in their view required, as its major conditions, a resumption of international trade and a rebuilding of the international credit structure through a substantial lowering of trade barriers; a stabilization of foreign exchanges, as the first stage in the re-establishment of an international gold standard; and a restoration of national financial solvency by the balancing of public budgets and the avoidance of fiscal inflation. International agreement along these lines and a clearly indicated disposition to embark upon appropriate action, accompanied by a clearing-up of the war debt controversy and an adjustment of outstanding political issues, were bound, in their opinion, to re-create confidence and to open the way for a rise in commodity prices as an instrument for restoring a balance between prices and costs.

In placing the results of their discussions before the governments, the experts prefaced their recommendations with the following warning:

It is necessary to emphasize the close inter-connection between the various elements of the problem. It will not, in our judgment, be possible to make substantial progress by piecemeal measures. A policy of "nibbling" will not solve this crisis. We believe that the governments of the world must make up their minds to achieve a broad solution by concerted action along the whole front. Action in the field of economic relations depends largely upon monetary and financial action, and vice versa. Concerted measures in both fields are essential if progress is to be made in either.

In short, there was general, though perhaps not unanimous, agreement upon three fundamental propositions: (1) that independent action by individual countries will not solve the economic difficulties of the world or even of such countries themselves; (2) that while credit policies are an important factor in the process of recovery, a rise in commodity prices can ultimately have the desired effect of re-establishing economic equilibrium only if it comes about as an accompaniment of general recovery; and (3) that the restoration of an international monetary standard, capable of providing stability of foreign exchanges, is an indispensable element in any program of recovery.

CHAPTER III

WASHINGTON: SHIFTS OF EMPHASIS

The program of action recommended by the Geneva experts did not constitute any sort of binding agreement among governments. Each remained free to decide for itself whether to act in accordance with this program or some other plan. Indeed, it was for the purpose of arriving at such decisions that the World Conference was being convoked. However, the experts felt it incumbent upon them to make the following suggestion to the governments to which they were reporting:

In stressing the necessity for concerted action, we do not wish to suggest that nothing can be accomplished before the conference meets. On the contrary, the success of the conference will depend in great measure upon the vigor with which the participating governments enter upon preliminary negotiations in the meantime. The prospects of substantial all-round success in the necessarily complex and multilateral conference discussions will be greatly enhanced if, in the intervening months, preliminary negotiations have cleared the way for reciprocal concessions.

Preliminary negotiations of this sort took place sporadically during the five months that elapsed between the meeting of the experts and the opening of the conference. The most important among them was a series of consultations between President Roosevelt and responsible statesmen of all the important nations, which began in Washington at the end of April and lasted into the early part of June. In these consultations the outstanding issues were surveyed, in the light of the experts' recommendations, as well as in the light of unfolding events and developing policies.

By comparison with the conditions which prevailed at the beginning of the year, the world's monetary situation during the period from January to June became vastly more complicated because of the banking panic in the United States, followed by America's departure from the gold standard and the development of a comprehensive program of domestic economic recovery. As a result of these great changes, not only did foreign exchange instability and uncertainty greatly increase, but the problem of restoring a stable international monetary standard became more difficult. Under the influence of these new factors, the whole approach to the work of the projected World Conference assumed a different aspect, and new monetary issues of paramount importance came into the foreground of public discussion.

I. AMERICA'S DEPARTURE FROM THE GOLD STANDARD

The abandonment of the gold standard by the United States was accomplished in two stages. First, gold redemption and export were suspended by Presidential proclamation in March. Second, a way was opened for the depreciation of the dollar in foreign exchange markets by the executive order of April 20, and authority for a reorganization of the whole monetary system was given to the President by the Act of Congress approved May 12. As a result, the American currency became irredeemable paper, and the foreign exchange value of the dollar became subject to fluctuation.

A. Suspension of Gold Redemption and Exports

The first step in the suspension of the gold standard was one of the emergency measures introduced by President Roosevelt immediately after he took office, for the purpose of meeting the acute banking difficulties which had arisen throughout the country just prior to his inauguration. By March 3 practically all banking institutions in the country had been closed, by the order of state authorities with respect to banks under their jurisdiction and of the Comptroller of the Currency with respect to national banks—authority having been granted to the Comptroller for this purpose by joint congressional resolutions of February 25 and March 3. In order to introduce uniformity and to centralize authority in dealing with this critical emergency, on March 6 the President proclaimed a national banking holiday which affected the Federal Reserve Banks as well as all other banking institutions. Specifically, all these institutions were forbidden—except by special permission of the Secretary of the Treasury, with the approval of the President—to "pay out, export, earmark, or permit the withdrawal or transfer in any manner or by any device whatsoever, of any gold or silver coin or bullion or currency." They were also forbidden to "pay out deposits, make loans or discounts, deal in foreign exchange, or transfer credits from the United States to any place abroad."

The national banking holiday was made operative through March 9. It was proclaimed by the President on the authority of a war-time measure, embodied in the Act of Congress of October 6, 1917, which still remained in effect. Under the same authority, a large number of regulations relating to various banking matters were issued by the Secretary of the Treasury.

On March 9, in response to a special message from the President, Congress passed an Act designed "to provide relief in the existing national emergency in banking." By this Act, all the measures taken by the President and the Secretary of the Treasury since March 4 under the authority of the Act of October 6, 1917, were approved and confirmed. Furthermore, the 1917 Act was amended in such a way as to empower the President, "during time of war or any other period of national emergency declared by the President," to "investigate, regulate, or prohibit, under such rules and regulations as he may prescribe, by means of licences or otherwise, any transactions in foreign exchange, transfers of credit between or payments by banking institutions as defined by the President, and export, hoarding, melting, or ear-marking of gold or silver coin or bullion or currency, by any person within the United States or any place sub-ject to the jurisdiction thereof." The Federal Reserve Act was amended by the insertion of a provision that

Whenever in the judgment of the Secretary of the Treasury such action is necessary to protect the currency system of the United States, the Secretary of the Treasury, in his discretion, may require any or all individuals, partnerships, associations, and corporations to pay and deliver to the Treasurer of the United States any or all gold coin, gold bullion, and gold certificates owned by such individuals, partnerships, associations, or corpora-tions.

Finally, the President was authorized, in periods of emergency, to place all member banks of the Federal Reserve system under complete regulation by the Sec-retary of the Treasury. All violations of the Act were made punishable by a fine of not more than $10,000, or imprisonment for a period of not more than ten years.

Under the authority of the new Act, on March 9 the President issued a new proclamation, extending the banking holiday indefinitely, "until further proclama-tion." On March 10 this was followed by an executive order which contained several extremely important provisions. The Secretary of the Treasury was empowered to re-open banks, under such conditions as he might prescribe. However, except by special order of the Secretary, no permission to re-open was to contain an authorization "to pay out any gold coin, gold bullion, or gold certificates," or "to allow withdrawal of any currency for hoarding." The re-opening institutions were also forbidden "to engage in any transactions in foreign exchange except such as may be undertaken for legitimate and normal business requirement, for reasonable traveling and other personal requirements, and for the fulfillment of contracts entered into prior to March 6, 1933." Finally, all exports of gold coin, bullion, or certificates were prohibited until further order, "except in accordance with regulations prescribed by or under license issued by the Secretary of the Treasury."

The executive order of March 10 constituted the formal suspension of the gold standard by the United States. It did not, however, result in any substantial depreciation of the dollar in foreign exchanges, nor in more than slight fluctuations in the dollar exchange rate. While the United States currency was no longer redeemable in gold and free gold exports were formally forbidden, gold could still be obtained under license for purposes of international transactions and, again under license, shipped abroad or earmarked for foreign account. At the same time, while foreign exchange transactions were placed under regulation, sufficient latitude was permitted by the exceptions to this general rule for normal international settlements to remain practically unobstructed. This fact, together with an adequately liberal administration of the gold licensing system and the psychological factors indicated below was mainly responsible for the stability of the dollar exchange during the second half of March and the first half of April. (See frontispiece chart.)

In these earlier regulations, the President and the Secretary of the Treasury did not avail themselves of the provision contained in the Act of March 9 which empowered them to demand delivery to the Treasurer of the United States of all privately held gold coin, bullion, and certificates. But on April 5 the President issued an executive order, giving effect to this provision by forbidding the hoarding of gold. Although the term "hoarding" was defined in the order as "the withdrawal and withholding of gold coin, gold bullion, and gold certificates from the recognized and customary channels of trade," it was, in reality, given the interpretation of involving the mere fact of possession of gold. Accordingly, it was ordered that "all persons (meaning individuals, partnerships, associations, or corporations) are hereby required to deliver on or before May 1, 1933, to a Federal Reserve Bank or a branch or agency thereof or to any member bank of the Federal Reserve system all gold coin, gold bullion, and gold certificates now owned by them or coming into their possession on or before April 28, 1933." Exception was made for reasonable amounts of the metal required for industrial use; for maximum individual holdings of $100, as well as for rare and unusual coins in any amount; for gold already placed under earmark; and for gold already licensed or held pending action on applications for licenses. It was likewise ordered that all persons acquiring possession of gold after April 28 must deliver it in the manner specified above "within three days after receipt thereof." Finally, all member banks were ordered to deliver to their respective Federal Reserve Banks all gold received or owned by them.

The next and in some respects the most vital step in the process of suspending the gold standard was represented by the executive order issued on April 20. By this order the partial embargo on gold exports imposed on March 10 was made absolute. Although the gold embargo provisions of the earlier order were merely reiterated and the Secretary of the Treasury was still empowered to license gold exports "with the approval of the President, for transactions which he may deem necessary to promote the public interest," notice was, in effect, served that no more gold would be released from the monetary stocks of the United States government.

The executive order of April 20 resulted in an immediate and substantial depreciation of the dollar exchange, as may be seen from the frontispiece chart. What happened was that, under the operation of the March order, the foreign exchange rate of the dollar was maintained by shipments of gold and the comparative freedom of foreign exchange transactions. The April order meant the abandoning of the dollar exchange to free fluctuations.

B. Gold and Dollar Exchange Position

In the Presidential proclamation of March 6, the reasons for declaring a national banking holiday were stated as follows:

Whereas there have been heavy and unwarranted withdrawals of gold and currency from our banking institutions for the purpose of hoarding; and

Whereas continuous and increasingly extensive speculative activity abroad in foreign exchanges has resulted in severe drains on the nation's stocks of gold; and

Whereas these conditions have created a national emergency. . . .

All subsequent measures, including the suspension of the gold standard on March 10 and the withdrawal of support from the dollar exchange on April 20, were taken for the purpose of meeting the national emergency as here defined.

Of the conditions officially announced as having been responsible for the national emergency represented by the banking crisis, by far the most important was the withdrawal and hoarding of paper currency, as may be seen from the charts on pages 44 and 45. The increased demand for notes between February 15 and March 4 amounted to 1,330 million dollars and more than half of this demand was made during the first three days of March. As a result, the volume of Federal Reserve notes expanded rapidly by more than 50 per cent.

The demand for gold coin and gold certificates, while much smaller in volume, was also abnormally intense. During the same period the gold (coin and certificates) in circulation increased by about 300 million dollars. However, this increase started from an unusually low level of gold circulation—the lowest point attained since 1923—and even on March 4 the total was under the level prevailing at the beginning of 1932 and far below the high point attained at the end of 1930.

The loss of gold to other countries was also substantial, but not at the moment of startling proportions. Between February 1 and March 4 the country's total stock of gold decreased by 305 million dollars. This amount was much smaller than had been the case on two previous recent occasions when there was a large efflux of gold from the United States. During May-June 1932, the gold stock decreased by 448 millions, and during September-October 1931, by 703 millions. The gold stock on March 4 was well above what it was in mid-summer of 1932, and was only slightly smaller than the average for the years 1928-29.

The decrease in the total gold stock and the loss of gold into circulation served, however, to diminish the monetary reserves of the Federal Reserve system, and

FEDERAL RESERVE GOLD HOLDINGS AND NOTES IN CIRCULATION, 1929-33[a]

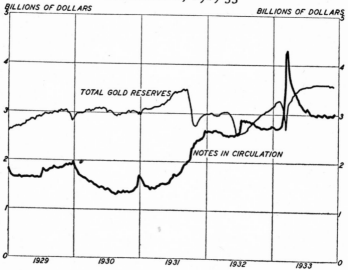

* Federal Reserve Board weekly figures for all Reserve Banks.

in this manner contributed to the rapid weakening of the country's monetary position. On February 1 the reserve ratio of the 12 Federal Reserve Banks combined was 65.6 per cent. By March 4 it dropped to 45.1 per cent, or perilously close to the statutory minimum.[1]

---

[1] The figures given here are from *Federal Reserve Bulletin*, April 1933, pp. 209-13 and 259-60.

Under the influence of the emergency measures, the technical monetary position improved almost as rapidly as it had deteriorated before. Paper currency, gold coins,

VOLUME OF MONEY OUTSTANDING, GOLD STOCKS, AND GOLD IN CIRCULATION IN THE UNITED STATES, 1919-33[a]

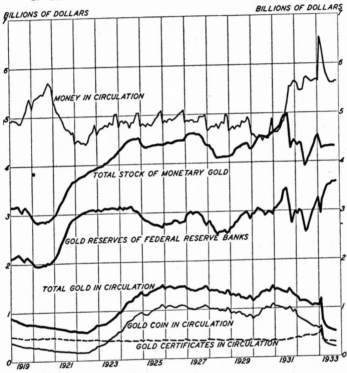

[a] Monthly figures from *Federal Reserve Bulletins.*

and gold certificates were restored to the banks in large amounts. As a result, note circulation declined, the reserves of the banks of issue increased, and the reserve ratio rose again above 60 per cent. This improvement continued into April.

Between March 4 and April 19 the total gold stock

changed from 4,333 million dollars to 4,313 millions. Thus the maintenance of the dollar exchange rate close to its gold parity over a period of more than five weeks, while requiring a certain amount of current gold movements into and out of the country, entailed a net loss of gold amounting to only 20 million dollars.

In the light of this improvement in the country's general monetary position and of the fact that the Treasury issued certificates of five and nine months' duration on March 16, payable as usual "in United States gold coin of the present standard of value," it was naturally assumed by the public in general that the suspension of the gold standard was to be merely an emergency measure, and that no change in the gold content of the dollar was in contemplation. Indeed, there is no evidence to show that the government at this juncture was seriously considering a reduction in the weight of the dollar.

The situation, however, underwent swift change during the first half of April. There was a rapidly developing movement in Congress for a program of currency inflation intended to raise prices rapidly, and outside of Congress there was also a strong organized movement for the devaluation of the dollar, with the same end in view. On April 20 there was introduced in Congress, with the approval of the President, an amendment to the farm relief bill, which made possible fundamentally significant changes in our monetary policy. The monetary provisions in this bill are numerous and varied in character; hence it is necessary to present them in some detail.

C. Authorized Changes in Monetary Policy

The Thomas amendment, including a series of important provisions proposed with reference to silver by

Senator Key Pittman of Nevada, became Title III of
the farm relief bill, and as such was enacted into law
when the whole measure was approved by the President on May 12. The monetary privisions of the Act,
with one exception, as we shall see, are permissive in
character, conferring upon the President power to take
action in his discretion.

1. Expansion of Federal Reserve credit. The President is authorized, at his discretion, to direct the Secretary of the Treasury to enter into an agreement with
the Federal Reserve Banks and the Federal Reserve
Board for an expansion of the volume of currency and
credit created by the Federal Reserve system. This is
to be accomplished in two ways: First, by ordinary open
market operations, involving the purchase by Federal
Reserve Banks of government securities from commercial banks and private individuals. The purpose of such
purchases would be to ease the credit position of banks
and the money market in general. Second, by an authorization to the Federal Reserve Banks to purchase
direct from the Treasury (in addition to government
securities bought in the open market) Treasury bills and
other obligations of the United States government, in
an aggregate amount of not more than 3 billion dollars.
These securities the Federal Reserve Banks could not
resell to the public, except by permission of the Secretary of the Treasury. This second provision would
make it easier for the government to finance budgetary
deficits.

This section of the Thomas amendment involves a new
grant of power, to the Treasury, rather than to the Federal Reserve system. It enables the Treasury to take the
initiative in arranging for an expansion of Federal Reserve credit. A new grant of power to the Federal Re-

serve system is contained in the provision under which, if such expansion should reduce the system's reserves below existing minimum reserve requirements—namely, 40 per cent gold against notes and 35 per cent in "lawful money" against demand deposits—the Federal Reserve Board is empowered to permit a suspension of these reserve requirements without incurring the penalties for such action provided in the Federal Reserve Act.[2]

2. *Greenbacks.* In the event that the Federal Reserve system should refuse to enter into such an agreement, or in the event that the President should decide that the creation of a still greater volume of currency was needed, he is authorized to avail himself of the Treasury note-issuing powers under the Act of February 25, 1862, which provided for the issuing of United States notes, commonly known as "greenbacks." The new Act stipulates that such notes should be "in the same size and of similar color to the Federal Reserve notes heretofore issued" and of similar denominations (from $1.00 to $10,000), *but that they should be used by the Treasury only for the purpose of retiring interest-bearing obligations of the United States government.* The maximum amount of this issue is fixed at 3 billion dollars, and an obligation is laid on the Secretary of the Treasury to retire the issue at the rate of 4 per cent annually of the amount outstanding.

3. *Changes in the monetary standard.* The modifications in this connection relate to both gold and silver coinage, to the gold standard, and to bimetalism. In fact, the provisions are so confused that it would appear that the President is simultaneously authorized to establish

---

[2] Such penalties consist of a graduated tax on all excess note issues and an obligation to raise the discount rate.

bimetalism at his discretion and obligated to maintain the single gold standard.

The President is given power to fix the gold content of the dollar at any number of grains that he sees fit, provided the present weight of 25.8 grains, 9/10ths fine, is not reduced by more than one half. Thereafter the gold dollar of the newly fixed weight would become the standard unit of value. The law then reiterates the provision of the Gold Standard Act of 1900 in which a duty is imposed on the Secretary of the Treasury to maintain all forms of currency at a parity with the standard gold unit. This clearly indicates an obligation to continue to maintain a monometallic gold standard.

On the other hand, the President is empowered to fix the weight of silver dollars "at a definite fixed ratio to the gold dollar," the choice of the ratio being left to his discretion. Having determined the relative metallic contents of gold and silver dollars, the President is further authorized to provide for unlimited coinage of both metals. This would clearly be bimetalism.

4. Silver certificates. The Act authorizes the President, for a period of six months from the date of its passage, to accept silver in payment of accounts owed by foreign governments to the United States in an aggregate amount of not over 200 million dollars and at a price of not more than 50 cents an ounce. Against any silver thus received, the Secretary of the Treasury is directed to issue silver certificates "to the total number of dollars for which such silver was accepted in payment of debts," the certificates to be used in payment of any obligations of the United States government.

The silver bullion is to be coined in such amounts as, in the judgment of the Secretary of the Treasury, would be required for the purpose of redeeming the certificates. It is also provided that "when any silver certificates issued under the provisions of this section are redeemed or received into the Treasury from any source whatsoever, and belong to the United States, they shall not be retired, cancelled, or destroyed, but shall be reissued, and paid out again, and kept in circulation."

5. *Change in legal tender powers.* In connection with the authorization of new issues of greenbacks, the Act provides that "such notes and all other coins and currencies heretofore or hereafter coined or issued under the authority of the United States shall be legal tender for all debts public and private." The wording of this provision led to a confusion of interpretation as to whether it would become applicable with respect to existing forms of currency *immediately* or only after new issues of greenbacks had been made. It was, however, soon officially made clear that the Act was to be interpreted as immediately changing the existing provisions with regard to the legal tender power of the various forms of currency. On June 5, as we shall presently see, the Act was amended to make this change specific.

Prior to this time, the only forms of United States currency which possessed full and unlimited legal tender power were gold coins and gold certificates, all other kinds of money being limited in this respect in varying degrees. This meant that gold coins and gold certificates could never be refused when offered, in any amount, in payment of any obligation, private or public. While the obligatory acceptance of other forms of money was legally limited either as to amount that could be offered or as to the nature of obligation to be settled, so long as all these other forms of money were redeemable in gold, the degree to which they were legal tender was a matter of no practical significance. But with the suspension of redemption—at least temporarily—it was felt that all forms of currency should be made full legal tender, in order to insure their free circulation.[3]

6. *Abolition of the gold clause.* For a long time it had been a common practice in this country to write into public and private bonds and other contracts (as a specific safeguard against changes in the monetary standard) a provision for payment "in gold coin of present degree of weight and fineness." But after the suspension of the gold standard, the question arose whether such contracts were enforceable, either through demand for gold coin or for additional sums in other forms of currency equal to the premium on gold. The Act of May 12 failed to clarify this issue either with respect to payments within the country or obligations held abroad. As regards the latter, however, it was officially announced on May 1 that gold export licenses for the purpose of meeting maturing obligations or interest coupons on United States securities held in other countries would be refused on the ground that "such export [of gold] would not be in the public interest."[4]

[3] In addition to gold coins and gold certificates, there are nine other forms of currency in the United States. Of these, silver dollars, silver certificates, and Treasury notes of 1890 were, prior to May 12, full legal tender, except where otherwise expressly stipulated in contract. United States notes, or greenbacks, were full legal tender, except for payment of import duties and of interest on the public debt, although in practice this last provision was not operative. The foregoing six kinds of currency were defined as "lawful money." Federal Reserve notes, Federal Reserve Bank notes, and national bank notes were not legal tender, and circulated at par because of their redeemability in gold. Fractional silver coins were legal tender for payments not exceeding $10, and minor coins for payments of not over 25 cents.

[4] It should be noted that other countries seldom had a gold clause in

In order to clear up existing confusion on this whole question, Congress, by a joint resolution introduced on May 26 at the request of the President and approved by him on June 5, announced the fulfillment of all existing "gold clause" contracts to be "against public policy"; prescribed that all existing obligations containing such a stipulation might be discharged in any form of legal tender currency; and declared that "no such provision shall be contained in or made with respect to any obligations hereafter incurred."

By the same resolution, the provision in the law of May 12 relating to legal tender powers was, in order to make it more specific, amended to read as follows:

All coins and currencies of the United States (including Federal Reserve notes and circulating notes of Federal Reserve Banks and national banking associations) heretofore or hereafter coined or issued, shall be legal tender for all debts, public and private, public charges, taxes, duties and dues.

D. Objectives and Control Provisions

The general purpose underlying the monetary provisions of the Act of May 12 was, as already indicated, to promote a rise in commodity prices. This basic objective was stated in the following terms by President Roosevelt, in his radio address of May 6, made while the Thomas amendment was under discussion in Congress:

The Administration has the definite objective of raising commodity prices to such an extent that those who have borrowed money will, on the average, be able to repay that money in the same kind of dollar which they borrowed. We do not seek to

---

contracts. Hence, when their currencies depreciated they proceeded, as a matter of course, to pay in the depreciated paper—not, however, without objection from foreign creditors.

let them get such a cheap dollar that they will be able to pay back a great deal less than they borrowed. In other words, we seek to correct a wrong and not to create another in the opposite direction. That is why powers are given to the Administration to provide, if necessary, for an enlargement of credit, in order to correct the existing wrong. These powers will be used when, as, and if it may be necessary to accomplish this purpose.

Some of the devices for bringing about a price rise by monetary action have been outlined in the preceding section. But the Act also contains a number of safeguard provisions which would limit the extent to which expansion of currency and credit might go. Maximum limits are set to the volume of direct sales of government obligations by the Treasury to the Federal Reserve Banks; to the amount of greenbacks and silver certificates to be issued by the Treasury; and to the reduction of the gold content of the dollar. Open market operations are left unlimited in scope, but the framers of the law clearly placed little reliance on their efficacy, since they provided so many substitutes for them.

However, the possibilities of expansion are so vast, even within these limitations, that it may be necessary for the Federal Reserve Board to exercise a restraining influence. With this in mind the two following provisions were inserted:

1) The Federal Reserve Board, with the approval of the Secretary of the Treasury, may require the Federal Reserve Banks to take such action as may be necessary, in the judgment of the Board and of the Secretary of the Treasury, to prevent undue credit expansion.

2) The Federal Reserve Board, upon the affirmative vote of not less than five of its members and with the approval of the President, may declare that an emergency exists by reason of credit expansion, and may by regulation during such emergency increase or decrease from time to time, in its own discretion, the

reserve balances required to be maintained against either demand or time deposits.

With reference to the second provision it should be borne in mind that, under the existing legislation, member banks are required to maintain minimum reserves, varying from 7 to 13 per cent, against demand deposits held by them, and of 3 per cent against time deposits. The volume of commercial credit extended by them is, in part, governed by these reserve requirements, and the right of the Federal Reserve Board to raise or lower these requirements is expected to have the effect of exercising a direct control over the volume of credit.

One further objective of the measures permitting the depreciation of the dollar exchange and of the provision for the reduction in the weight of the dollar remains to be mentioned. In the Thomas amendment the President is explicitly given authority to expand currency and credit and to reduce the gold content of the dollar whenever he finds, upon investigation, that "the foreign commerce of the United States is adversely affected by reason of the depreciation in the value of the currency of any other government or governments in relation to the present standard value of gold"; that "an expansion of credit is necessary to secure by international agreement a stabilization at proper levels of the currencies of various governments"; or, finally, "in case the government of the United States enters into an agreement with any government or governments under the terms of which the ratio between the value of gold and other currency issued by the United States and by any such government or governments is established." This was clearly designed to give the President bargaining powers in view of the projected international negotiations, particularly in connection with the London Conference.

II. WASHINGTON CONSULTATIONS

Shortly before public policy in the United States had taken the sharp and decisive turn which has just been described, invitations were issued to the heads of all important governments for informal consultations in Washington on the subject of the outstanding international problems and the work of the forthcoming World Conference. Events, however, moved with such rapidity that the promulgation of the executive order of April 20 and the introduction in Congress of the Thomas amendment took place while Prime Minister MacDonald, representing Great Britain, and M. Edouard Herriot, representing France, were on the Atlantic Ocean, on their way to Washington. Upon their arrival in this country, therefore, the European statesmen were confronted with a situation which was different, in vital respects, from what it had been at the time the invitations were accepted. These changes had a profound influence on the character of the consultations and the subsequent course of international discussion in the monetary sphere.

The principal statesmen with whom President Roosevelt conferred were the following: Prime Minister MacDonald of Great Britain, M. Herriot of France, Finance Minister Guido Jung of Italy, Dr. Hjalmar Schacht of Germany, Prime Minister Bennett of Canada, Viscount Kikujiro Ishii of Japan, Finance Minister T. V. Soong of China, Ambassador Le Breton of Argentina, Señor J. F. deAssis-Brasil of Brazil, and Finance Minister Alberto Pani of Mexico. Except for certain questions which were discussed jointly by President

Roosevelt, Mr. MacDonald, and M. Herriot, the consultations were of an individual character, the President conferring in turn with each of the visiting statesmen. At the termination of each conference, a joint statement was issued by the President and his particular conferee.

These joint statements recorded in general terms the results of the consultations. The conferences, being merely of an exploratory character, the pronouncements did not contain any agreed program of policy and action, but rather observations which the statesmen concerned considered useful for general public knowledge. Nevertheless, the statements were highly indicative of the trends of thought which were, at the time, actuating public policy in various countries.

Needless to say, only a small part of the discussions found reflection in the joint statements. President Roosevelt and his visitors surveyed all the outstanding issues of the day. But it was perfectly clear from the public pronouncements that the problem of commodity prices dominated all of the conversations. This was inevitable, in view of the fact that the basic policy of the United States had become directed toward price-raising as the supreme objective. However, the insistence on a need for raising commodity prices was presented, in the different joint statements, with significant variations of formulation.

The Roosevelt-MacDonald statement contained the following passage:

Our discussions on the questions facing the World Economic Conference were not designed to result in definite agreements, which must be left to the conference itself. But they showed that our two governments were looking with a like purpose and a close similarity of method at the main objectives of the conference, and were impressed by the vital necessity of assuring international agreements for their realization in the interests of the peoples of all countries. The practical measures which are required for their realization were analyzed and explored.

The necessity for an increase in the general level of commodity prices was recognized as primary and fundamental. To this end simultaneous action needs to be taken both in the economic and in the monetary field. Commercial policies have to be set to a new orientation. There should be constructive effort to moderate the network of restrictions of all sorts by which commerce is at present hampered, such as excessive tariffs, quotas, exchange restrictions, etc. Central banks should by concerted action provide an adequate expansion of credit and every means should be used to get the credit thus created into circulation. Enterprise must be stimulated by creating conditions favorable to business recovery, and governments can contribute by the development of appropriate programs of capital expenditure.

It should be noted that here an overwhelming emphasis was laid on price recovery, and that the stabilization of foreign exchanges was not mentioned among the measures designed to promote a rise in commodity prices. The monetary question was treated in the following terms:

The ultimate re-establishment of equilibrium in the international exchange should also be contemplated. We must, when circumstances permit, re-establish an international monetary standard which will operate successfully without depressing prices and avoid the repetition of the mistakes which have produced such disastrous results in the past. In this connection, the question of silver, which is of such importance in trade with the Orient, was discussed, and proposals were tentatively suggested for the improvement of its status.

The various elements in the recovery program were given somewhat different emphasis in the American-French statement, where they were treated as follows:

The government of the United States and the government of France have been able already to announce their full agreement in regard to the necessity of a prompt meeting of this conference, the object of which must be to bring about a rapid revival of world activity and the raising of world prices by diminishing all sorts of impediments to international commerce such as tariffs, quotas and exchange restrictions, and by the re-establishment of a normal financial and monetary situation. . . . We have studied monetary problems and the different methods possible for a co-ordination of central bank policy; the remedies which might be brought forward to attack the menacing problem of unemployment and the stagnation of business by the execution of programs of public works to be carried out by the different governments by such methods as are within their means; the effects of the depression on silver and the different methods proposed to improve its status.

In this formulation, an equal stress was laid on "a rapid revival of world activity" and "the raising of world prices" as joint objectives, and "the re-establishment of a normal monetary situation" was brought in as one of the indispensable conditions for achieving these objectives.

A still different emphasis and a definite introduction of the stabilization of foreign exchange into the program of recovery were contained in the American-Italian statement:

We are in agreement that a fixed measure of exchange values must be re-established in the world, and we believe that this measure must be gold. The entire problem of raising world prices and restoring the opportunity to work to men and women who today wish to work and can find no employment is a unit. It must be attacked as a unit. Along with the measures which must be taken to restore normal conditions in the financial and monetary field and stability in international exchanges, must go hand in hand measures for removing the obstacles to the flow of international commerce.

These were not merely differences of phraseology. They went to the very root of the matter. They showed clearly that Great Britain and the principal gold countries were still fundamentally as far apart as they were at the beginning of the year on the question of the relation of prices and foreign exchanges to the program of recovery. The British were still adhering to their view that an adjustment of prices to costs through a rise in the former must precede any attempt to stabilize foreign exchanges, while the gold countries continued to maintain that the re-establishment of foreign exchange stability is one of the indispensable factors in bringing about any price-cost adjustment. The differences also indicated that the official policy of the United States on this vital issue, which was in line with the position of the gold countries at the beginning of the year, was no longer definite and distinct.

On the other hand, it was apparent after the Washington consultations that the problem of price-raising would dominate the World Conference itself. Clearly, the recommendations of the Geneva experts in this respect did not prove to be acceptable to at least some of the principal statesmen of the world.

Moreover, a method of price-raising which was never seriously considered at Geneva appeared to have come to the fore, although no reflection of it was found in any of the joint statements. According to reports current at the time, there was serious discussion of a proposal, sponsored by the United States and vigorously opposed by the gold countries, that the whole world should embark upon a "cheaper money" policy, not only through a vigorous and concerted program of credit expansion and the stimulation of business enterprise by means of public works, but also through a simultaneous devaluation, by a fixed percentage, of all currencies which were still at their pre-depression parities.

Another departure from the experts' program was in connection with silver. This issue emerged to assume a place of much greater prominence than it had been given before. It was mentioned in every important joint statement in terms forecasting definite action with respect to it.

On one subject the statesmen conferring in Washington declared themselves unequivocally in full agreement. That was the imperative necessity for the World Conference to meet at an early date and to proceed rapidly to necessary agreement. The determination to act along these lines found its strongest expression in the statement issued by President Roosevelt and the spokesman for the Italian government, in which it was presented as follows:

The world faces a crisis of the first magnitude. If normal life is to be resumed, the World Economic Conference must be made a success. It must not only meet soon, but come to its conclusions quickly. The task is so complex and difficult that, unless it is approached by all nations with the fullest and sincerest desire to arrive at a result, the conference cannot succeed. But the other course before the world is clearly an increase in economic warfare, and all nations must co-operate in attempting to avoid this alternative.

It was in Washington, in the course of the Roosevelt-MacDonald-Herriot conversations, that decision was reached to convoke the conference for June 12. On April 29 the organizing committee, set up by the Council of the League of Nations for the purpose of arranging the conference, met in London and formally announced June 12 as the opening date. Intensive technical preparations for the parley were immediately begun.

III. DOMESTIC VERSUS INTERNATIONAL PROGRAM OF RECOVERY

While the statesmen conferring in Washington were giving public expression to their determination to convoke the World Conference at an early date and to bring it to a speedy and successful termination, an important change of emphasis in connection with another vital issue was becoming apparent. The principal impetus of this shift also came from Washington. That was the question whether the problem of recovery should be approached primarily as an international or a national one. The Geneva experts laid special emphasis on the former, since they saw in the constantly growing tendency toward a wider and deeper disruption of international trade and financial relations, resulting mainly from independent national attempts at remedying economic difficulties, the principal cause of the continuing depression. But here, as elsewhere, the experts' analysis failed to coincide with political expediency in at least some of the important countries.

During the months of March and April a violent controversy on this general subject excited public opinion in Great Britain. It centered around the character of the British budget for the current year, with an important group, led by Mr. John Maynard Keynes, making a vigorous attempt to convince the government that public finances should be used as an instrument of national recovery. The specific proposal was that the balance between public revenues and expenditures, established with great difficulty during the preceding year, should be deliberately broken as a means of stimulating a resumption of economic activity. It was urged that the government should either reduce taxation, without decreasing expenditures, and in this manner stimulate business enterprise, or borrow for the purpose of inaugurating a program of public works, or do both. While Mr. Keynes' original proposal advocated concerted action of this sort in all the important countries, and while he repeatedly expressed himself as preferring international action to action by individual countries, nevertheless, recognizing the difficulties which stood in the way of an international program, he and his associates urged that, for the moment at any rate, such a use of the government budget as a "means to prosperity" should be made by individual countries, specifically by their own.

These proposals were emphatically rejected by the British government. In announcing on April 25 his own and his colleagues' determination to maintain budgetary equilibrium, the British Chancellor of the Exchequer solemnly declared their belief that a balanced budget, as a stabilizer of public confidence, was a more potent instrument of recovery than a deliberately unbalanced budget designed to act as a stimulant to business enterprise. He also re-emphasized his previously expressed conviction that a rise in commodity prices, which, he agreed, was indispensable to recovery, must, in order to be really beneficial, be international in character.

On the other hand, the doctrine of national recovery, as a starting point for a general upward trend, received increasing support in influential circles in the United States. The idea was becoming more and more prevalent that while attempts should be made to achieve international agreement as far as possible, the principal emphasis should be on domestic programs of recovery within individual nations. This idea was reflected in President Roosevelt's appeal to the heads of 54 nations, dispatched on May 16, when he said:

The World Economic Conference will meet soon and must come to its conclusions quickly. The world cannot await deliberations long drawn out. The conference must establish order in place of the present chaos by a stabilization of currencies, by freeing the flow of world trade, and by international action to raise price levels. It must, in short, supplement individual domestic programs for economic recovery by wise and considered international action.

The last sentence of this passage was of great significance. International action was clearly subordinated to domestic programs, the latter, as we have seen, having been already defined in terms of a rapidly induced rise in the domestic price level. More specific emphasis upon the pre-eminence of domestic programs of recovery was given by Professor Raymond Moley in a radio address on May 20, when he said:

It should not be expected that the conference itself is going to be able to lay out a plan for a series of international measures which will bring about the alleviation of economic difficulties all over the world. The action of an international conference which attempted to bring about cures for these difficulties solely by concerted international measures would necessarily result in failure. In large part the cures for our difficulties lie within ourselves. Each nation must set its own house in order, and a meeting of representatives of all the nations is useful in large part only to co-ordinate in some measure these national activities. Beyond this there are relatively few remedies which might be called international remedies.

The question whether the principal emphasis should be on international or national remedies was clearly of far-reaching importance in determining the basic criteria in the work of the conference. In either case there was bound to be a clash of views and policies, and the problem was whether the task of the conference would consist mainly in attaining international agreement on a program of world recovery, or in working out plans for co-ordinating, more or less, independent national programs. It so happened that the first and most important clash of this sort, which quickly brought the conference to an impasse, occurred in the monetary field.

CHAPTER IV

LONDON: CLASH OF POLICIES
AND IMPASSE

The World Monetary and Economic Conference opened in an atmosphere of uncertainty and apprehension. Officially the experts' Annotated Agenda continued to be the basis of discussion, but it was already clear, after the Washington consultations, that the program of action on which the conference would center its attention would be substantially different from that recommended at Geneva. The representatives of 64 nations gathering in London could only guess the precise direction of events. The possibility of a clash between national and international remedies, which was always present, assumed ever greater proportions as public policy in the United States, still in the process of formation, was rapidly developing in terms of an increasing emphasis on the former. Moreover, several immediate issues loomed on the horizon, overshadowing everything else.

In all discussions of the conference, prior to its actual convocation, it was repeatedly emphasized that an armistice must prevail in three major fields of international economic relations if the parley was to proceed successfully with its huge task. These were commercial policy, war debts, and currencies.

With respect to commercial policy, it was generally felt that no discussion of the problem of removal or mitigation of trade barriers would be fruitful unless the conference was free from the risk of sudden and important shifts of national trade policies. In order to meet this situation, the principal nations of the world, on the initiative of the United States, had, before the conference convened, agreed to a customs truce arrangement, which was open to adherence by other nations.

With respect to the war debts, it had been generally recognized that they should not, and properly could not, constitute a subject for conference discussion. But semi-annual instalments were falling due on June 15, and the debtor governments had repeatedly urged the government of the United States to agree, if not to a discussion of the problem before the conference or parallel with it, at least to an adjournment of the whole question for the duration of the parley, through a moratorium on the payments immediately falling due. This topic was touched upon during the Washington consultations, and special Roosevelt-MacDonald and Roosevelt-Herriot statements were issued on the subject, in which it was announced that "after the Prime Minister's departure, these conversations can well continue in London and Washington," and similarly that "these conversations may be continued in Paris and in Washington after M. Herriot has had an opportunity to report to the French government." But when the conference opened, the matter had advanced no further.

The war debt question was removed from the sphere of immediate public discussion when the American government accepted small token payments in silver from Great Britain, Italy, and several smaller debtors, at the same time giving its consent to an official review of the whole debt problem at some future date. However, while after June 15 the war debt problem no longer troubled the conference, the atmosphere surrounding the parley had been definitely made worse by the tension of the preceding three days and by the fact that Prime Minister MacDonald, as president of the conference, had felt it necessary, because of domestic political considerations, to refer to the debts in his opening speech.[1]

The question of currencies and foreign exchanges had also been discussed at Washington, when the need for a currency truce in the form of a temporary *de facto* stabilization of the principal foreign exchanges was urged, especially by M. Herriot, as an indispensable accompaniment of the customs truce. In the same manner as the debt problem, this question was left open after the Washington consultations, but on the eve of the conference steps were taken to reach an agreement with respect to it, thus insuring that during the course of the conference there would be no sudden alterations in national monetary policies.

The conference opened, therefore, in the midst of private American-British-French negotiations for a currency truce. The failure of these negotiations, which occurred within a few days after they began, had, as we shall see, a decisive effect on the work of the conference.

I. THE BREAKDOWN OF CURRENCY TRUCE NEGOTIATIONS

The negotiations for a currency truce, upon which the Treasury and central bank representatives of the

---

[1] Mr. MacDonald's statement on the war debts, which has frequently been incorrectly quoted, was as follows: "Behind the subjects I have just mentioned is another in the front rank of importance. It cannot be dealt with here, because obviously this conference is not constituted in such a way as to enable it to consider and settle the matter. I refer to the question of the war debts, which must be dealt with before every obstacle to general recovery has been removed, and it must be taken up without delay by the nations concerned. Lausanne has to be completed, and this vexed question settled once for all in the light of present world conditions."

United States, Great Britain, and France were engaged in London just before and just after the opening of the conference, involved fundamentally a decision on the part of the three governments concerned to bring the foreign exchange rates of their respective currency units into a condition of relative stability. Of the three countries, France was still on a full gold standard, and her part in the truce was to consist of continued adherence to that standard. Great Britain had maintained the sterling exchange rate approximately stable in terms of gold since the month of February, through the operation of the Exchange Equalization Account, and her contribution was to be an undertaking to continue doing so. The United States alone—since April 20—had had a freely fluctuating exchange rate, and her undertaking was to take the form of establishing machinery for confining the oscillations of the dollar exchange within comparatively narrow limits.

The task of the exchange experts negotiating in London was to work out a scheme of international co-operation that would facilitate action by individual countries. Involved in such co-operation was agreement upon: (1) the character of the technical collaboration among the three central banks necessary for the purpose of minimizing the effects of speculative influences on the foreign exchanges; (2) the ratios at which the dollar and the pound would, for the duration of the truce, be stabilized in terms of the French franc, the only gold currency, and thus with respect to each other; and (3) the limits within which the two non-gold currencies would be permitted to deviate from the basic ratios.

There were two principal alternatives with respect to central banking collaboration. One was the creation of a joint, tri-partite equalization fund, and the other the operation of individual equalization mechanisms by each of the countries, with the three central banks helping each other in every appropriate way without operating jointly. The American representatives were leaning toward the first alternative, while the French favored the second.

The problem of basic ratios was a matter for agreement between the governments of the United States and Great Britain. The former desired to narrow the already existing gap between the pound and the dollar, while the latter wished to maintain as large a differential as possible. Differences on the question of deviations from the basic ratios agreed upon lay between France's conviction that the margin should be as near as possible to the "gold points," which normally represent deviations of less than 1 per cent either way, and the desire of the non-gold countries for a much wider margin, somewhere in the neighborhood of 5 per cent.

In addition to these disagreements on technical details—which were difficult, though far from impossible of adjustment—there were also differences on much more basic issues. Great Britain and France stood committed to an anti-inflationist policy, and they felt that a similar policy on the part of the United States was indispensable to the functioning of the truce arrangement, on the ground that inflationist measures were likely to cause pressure on the exchange rates with which no equalization mechanism could cope. They therefore asked for a promise from President Roosevelt that for a specified period (three months was suggested at the time) he would refrain from making use of the permissive monetary powers granted him by the Act of May

12. The President did not find it possible to make such a promise. A compromise was attempted which involved a promise by the United States not to resort to inflation, unless a break occurred in the then continuing rise of commodity prices; but this did not prove to be acceptable.[2]

The limelight of public interest and discussion, during the opening days of the conference, even while the war debt issue was prominently in the foreground, was concentrated on the currency negotiations. In the absence of any official information as to the course of the negotiations, rumors and semi-authentic reports flew thick and fast. By being featured in the press, they caused fluctuations in the exchange rate of the dollar and created a general feeling of nervousness, especially in the stock and commodity markets of the United States, which were at that time in the midst of a speculative boom.

On June 15 a rise occurred in the exchange value of the dollar, and on the same day the prices of securities in New York broke sharply. A somewhat smaller decline was shown also by some of the important commodity prices. Although both price curves turned upward again when the dollar exchange began to fall the very next day, all these gyrations were attributed largely to the effects of rumors that a currency stabilization agreement was about to be reached, or had, indeed, already been achieved.

As a result, President Roosevelt ordered the London exchange stabilization negotiations discontinued. At the same time, it was announced in official American quarters that, in the opinion of the United States govern-

---

[2] In the absence of any official statements on the subject of currency truce negotiations, this account of what took place is based primarily upon the author's conversations in London at the time.

ment, any attempt at even temporary stabilization of the foreign exchanges was premature. On June 22 the American delegation to the conference issued an official statement, which read as follows:

> The American government at Washington finds that measures of temporary stabilization now would be untimely. The reason why it is considered untimely, is because the American government feels that its efforts to raise prices are the most important contribution it can make, and that anything that would interfere with these efforts and possibly cause a violent price recession would harm the conference more than the lack of an immediate agreement for temporary stabilization.

The negotiations for a currency truce were thus abruptly brought to an end. The conference got under way, in spite of this initial failure, but its work was at all points dominated by the continuing uncertainty and instability in the domain of foreign exchanges. A second and much less ambitious attempt was made two weeks later to reach agreement on this vital issue, but it also failed, as we shall presently see.

II. RESURGENCE OF PRICE CONTROVERSY

After the first week of its session, which was devoted to general discussion and was dominated by the war debt controversy and the first currency truce negotiations, the London Conference settled down to its task by creating two main commissions, the monetary and financial, and the economic. No sooner was this done than the currency question flared up again in connection with the chairmanship of the Monetary and Financial Commission, the point at issue being whether a representative of a gold or a non-gold country should be chosen to head the commission. This issue was finally settled by the appointment of Mr. James M. Cox, vice-

chairman of the American delegation, as president of
the commission, and of M. Georges Bonnet, the French
minister of finance, as the commission's *rapporteur*.

The Monetary and Financial Commission divided into
two sub-commissions, one of which was to consider "immediate measures of financial reconstruction," and the
other, "permanent measures for the re-establishment
of an international monetary standard." The allocation
of topics between the two sub-commissions showed clearly that the first was to deal with monetary policy, and
the second with technical matters.

The first sub-commission had the following items on
its agenda: credit policy, price levels, limitation of monetary fluctuations, foreign exchange control, international
indebtedness (referring to private debts alone), and resumption of international lending. The work began with
the consideration of the first two items, and it was on the
question of commodity prices in relation to monetary
policies that a major clash of national viewpoints developed from the very outset and deadlocked the whole
conference effort.

A. Debate on Credit and Prices

The sub-commission followed the rule which had
been adopted for the conference as a whole, that each
topic should be discussed on the assumption that all other
questions bearing on it, directly or indirectly, would be
satisfactorily resolved. Hence in the discussion of credit
and prices it was thought possible to rule out the consideration of such vital issues as commercial policies and
even the ultimate character of monetary organization.
The sub-commission attempted to narrow down its task
to the immediate relationship between price levels and

credit policies, and, in order to provide a basis for the discussion, the British delegation introduced the following draft resolution:

1. It is essential to bring about a recovery in the world level of wholesale commodity prices sufficient to yield an economic return to the producer of primary commodities and to restore equilibrium between costs of production and prices generally.

2. In order to obtain recovery in world prices, monetary action is one of the essential factors. The fundamental monetary conditions of recovery of prices are that deflation should cease, that cheap and plentiful credit should be made available, and that its circulation should be actively encouraged.

3. The central banks of the principal countries should undertake to co-operate with a view to securing these conditions and should announce their intention of pursuing vigorously a policy of cheap and plentiful money by open market operations.

In the debate on this draft resolution, there was no disagreement on the proposition that a recovery in the level of wholesale prices was desirable. But there was much criticism of the formulation of the whole question as given in the resolution, on the ground of excessive vagueness. There was also a sharp difference of opinion on the efficacy of monetary means for the purpose of raising prices, as well as an even more pronounced divergence of views regarding whether or not any monetary measures would represent constructive instruments of general economic recovery in the absence of foreign exchange stability—a subject which was deliberately omitted from the British draft.

The phrase "that deflation should cease" in particular aroused distinct misgivings in the minds of many of the speakers. The Dutch and the Czechoslovak representatives expressed their fears that it might easily be interpreted to imply an advocacy of deliberately unbalanced budgets and even of fiscal inflation. The Japanese representative was of the opinion that too much emphasis was being placed on credit expansion and too little stress on the dangers of inflation.

The efficacy of monetary measures for the purpose of raising prices was questioned by spokesmen for a number of countries. The Swiss representative expressed the opinion that "the expansion of credit should be a consequence of recovery, not a cause." The Italian representative thought that easy credit can be useful only as "a secondary force to set in motion a wider and brisker exchange of goods and services," and that "to put one's faith in immediate measures for augmenting the volume of money and credit might lead to a speculative boom followed by an even worse slump." To drive his point home, he used the following illustration:

> Credit is like water in a reservoir: if the water is spread over a field gradually, by an efficient system of irrigation, it would prove a fertilizing and energizing force; but a hasty and unregulated flood would lead to destructive results.

The restoration of confidence was stressed as the primary requirement in the process of price recovery, and the point was particularly emphasized that the foundation of such a restoration of confidence must be the reestablishment of stable monetary conditions. The principal spokesman for this point of view was the representative of France, who argued that of the two kinds of hoarding, which constitute the most striking manifestations of lack of confidence, only one—the hoarding of currency—can be combated by means of monetary uncertainty. He maintained, however, that even here the victory would be illusory, since, he insisted, the forcing of such hoarded money into the channels of trade by means of monetary uncertainty would merely represent a new form of hoarding: "hoarding in kind would take the place of hoarding of media of payment." But there is another kind of hoarding, the elimination of which is of paramount importance to economic recovery. That is the reluctance of investors to part with their available funds. On this point he said:

No durable recovery of consumption and trade is possible without re-creating the sense of security—political, economic, and monetary. . . . Who would be prepared to lend, with the fear of being repaid in depreciated currency always before his eyes? Who would find the capital for financing vast programs of economic recovery and abolition of unemployment, as long as there is a possibility that economic struggles would be transported to the monetary field? Wide fluctuations of the exchanges do not merely imperil national currencies or national economies; they may shake to its foundations the whole system of modern society, which is based on credit. In a word, without stable currency there can be no lasting confidence; while the hoarding of capital continues, there can be no solution.

No American representative took part in the debate on the British draft resolution, but immediately after the close of that debate, the American delegation formally introduced its own draft resolution on price levels and credit policy, which constituted a clear expression of the American point of view. The American draft, like the British, omitted all reference to currency stability, but it went far beyond the earlier document in precision as to the scope and character of the monetary and financial measures to be undertaken for the purpose of raising commodity prices and bringing about an expansion of business activity and increased employment.

The basic theory underlying the American proposal embodied two main postulates. The first was that "abundant credit and wise encouragement of private enterprise

through government expenditure are essential in bringing about an improvement in prices and an increase of
business activity." The second was that "such government expenditure shall not necessarily be included in the
budget for recurring expenses, but may properly be financed by borrowing, provided that the service of government debt so incurred is taken care of in a balanced
budget for recurring expenses."

It was proposed, therefore, that all the nations participating in the conference should agree to arrange for
a close co-operation between governments and between
their respective central banks with a view to "the carrying out of a policy of making credit abundantly and
readily available to sound enterprise," by means of open
market operations or any other practicable devices. It
was further proposed that "an acceleration of the process
of recovery should be sought by means of a synchronized
program of governmental expenditure in the different
countries along parallel lines," with the proviso that "it
is not the sense of this resolution that all nations should
agree necessarily to attack the problem in the same way,
but rather that the efforts already being made by many
nations should be co-ordinated and that other nations
should be stimulated to make similar efforts."

For the purpose of carrying out this agreement, it
was proposed (1) that a meeting of central bank representatives should immediately be assembled in London, and (2) that the conference should appoint a committee "to study the various methods of governmental
expenditure which have been in use or under consideration by the various nations, with a view toward making
a report to be sent to each of the nations for its guidance in working out its own program in the future."

This American proposal was not intended for public discussion by the sub-commission, but rather for the guidance of a special drafting committee, set up by the sub-commission for the purpose of attempting to prepare a generally acceptable draft resolution on the subject under consideration, taking into account the differences of views that had emerged from the debate. Such a committee was duly set up. It met only once, and then, in the language of the final report of the sub-commission, "the working of this committee was deferred in view of certain events affecting the possibility of reaching, for the time being, full agreement on the terms of resolutions on the subject."

The "certain events" mentioned here had reference to the repercussions of the message sent to the conference by President Roosevelt early in July, which will be discussed presently. But even without that development, it was perfectly clear that the conference had reached a parting of the ways on the fundamental question whether recovery was possible without an antecedent price rise. This price controversy, which proved to be the major issue in the work of the Preparatory Commission of Experts, emerged to the surface of the conference in the form of a still more acute and irreconcilable divergence of views and policies.

B. Three Groups at the Conference

The conference divided into three more or less definite groups, in accordance with their attitude on the price question. These were (1) the United States; (2) France and the other gold countries; and (3) Great Britain, supported mainly by her Dominions.

The United States was committed to a program of

raising commodity prices by monetary means. This was evident from the abandonment of the dollar to foreign exchange fluctuations, the new monetary legislation, and the policy of credit expansion through such means as open market operations and low interest rates. Stabilization of exchanges was presumably to be deferred until an adequate price rise had occurred.

In addition, the United States was embarking upon a comprehensive program for stimulating economic activity, which was expected to result in an added impetus to an upward movement of prices and in increased employment. Certain important parts of this program required large outlays of public funds, to be derived from borrowing. The budget was to be considered balanced if provision was made by means of taxes for interest and amortization charges on any new loans that might be incurred.

The program was conceived mainly in terms of determined action by individual countries in the directions indicated. Its international aspects were to consist of mutual stimulation and of assistance by countries with adequate financial resources of countries unable to proceed with the necessary measures. The program also envisaged an international co-ordination of action, directed mainly toward preventing national price levels from getting too far out of line with each other.

Of the countries represented in London, Sweden alone was lending a large measure of support to the American point of view. There was, however, an important difference between the positions of the two countries: the American program called for a rapid and substantial rise of the wholesale price level—the slogan, "back to 1926 prices," having already become widespread in the United States; the Swedish government inclined toward a slow and relatively small rise.

Opposed to the American position stood most of the continental countries of Europe, mainly those still on the gold standard. As has already been indicated in connection with the debate on the British resolution, they rejected the doctrine that price-raising should be the primary instrument in the recovery process, and they expressed grave doubts concerning the efficacy or desirability of monetary action as a means of recovery, irrespective of the type of action employed. The most important point on which they definitely parted company with the American position, however, was the utilization of a deliberate expansion of public outlays and of exchange instability as means to this end.

They pointed out that as a result of their disastrous fiscal experience during the post-war years, the public generally in their countries has come to recognize that unless all outlays, whatever their purpose and designation, are covered by current receipts, the budget is in fact unbalanced and that currency inflation inevitably ensues. Having with great difficulty—and in some cases with heavy sacrifices—won back to a condition of fiscal equilibrium, and having already seen that equilibrium destroyed by the depression, the governments of these countries expressed frank fears that to push their fiscal affairs, vigorously and deliberately, in the direction of a further lack of balance between income and outgo would bring them once more to utter disaster.

Similarly, with respect to currencies, almost all of them had passed through periods of depreciation and foreign exchange instability. They were convinced that the results of these bitter experiences were too fresh in the minds of their peoples for any deliberate action in the direction of bringing about a recurrence of these condition not to disrupt confidence and precipitate panic. They felt that this would be the case, no matter for what ultimately desirable purposes such an effort might be undertaken. Hence their insistence that currency depreciation should be ruled out as an instrument of price-raising policy and that clear evidence of this should be provided by at least a temporary stabilization of the principal foreign exchanges.

Between these two groups was Great Britain, supported mainly by her Dominions. The British position, as set forth in the resolution quoted on page 72, and expounded at length on several occasions by the British Chancellor of the Exchequer, was much nearer the American on the question of the primary importance of price-raising as a means to recovery than was that of the gold countries, but it was much nearer the latter than the former on the acceptability of some of the instruments of policy urged by the United States. The British government was pinning its faith mainly to cheap and plentiful credit. It was lukewarm on the question of public works, and, in conformity with its previously announced policy, strongly insistent upon fiscal equilibrium, with national budgets balanced and fiscal inflation rigorously avoided.

On the currency problem it had modified its view somewhat since the beginning of the year and was occupying a half-way position: the British government agreed with the American that the re-establishment of an international monetary standard and the definite fixation of the national monetary units should be deferred until an adequate rise had occurred in commodity prices.

But it was also in agreement with the governments of the gold countries in believing that ultimately the world's monetary organization should be based on a restored international gold standard and that a currency truce, in the form of a temporary stabilization of the principal foreign exchanges, was indispensable to effective work at the conference.[3]

III. PRESIDENT ROOSEVELT'S MESSAGE TO THE CONFERENCE

A second and final attempt to reconcile these differences of views on the currency question and to reach a compromise agreement that would enable the conference to proceed with its other numerous and complicated tasks, was made at the end of June. The initiative came from the gold countries, which were becoming increasingly alarmed with regard to their monetary position. The uncertainty prevailing at the conference was exercising a disorganizing effect on the gold exchanges, and the feeling was becoming widespread that the countries still on the gold standard were bound before long to be forced off gold. There was a steady flight of capital from these countries and adverse speculation against their currencies, which were causing substantial outflow of gold. The two countries particularly affected were Holland and Switzerland, which were generally regarded to be in a particularly vulnerable position. The former lost 12 per cent of her gold reserves during the month of June, and the latter, over 10 per cent. The other important gold countries—France, Italy, and Belgium—were similarly affected, though in a lesser degree.

[3] For the official summaries of the London proceedings, see *Journal of the Monetary and Economic Conference* (League of Nations publication).

The governments of these countries felt that this situation could be corrected if the monetary uncertainty at the conference were removed. Accordingly, at their request, a series of private consultations took place among representatives of the important nations, and plans were discussed for the issuing of a joint declaration on monetary policy, with special reference to the gold standard and the fluctuations of foreign exchanges. The text of such a declaration was finally drafted and read as follows:

I. The undersigned governments agree that:

a) it is in the interests of all concerned that stability in the international monetary field be attained as quickly as practicable;

b) that gold should be re-established as the international measure of exchange value, it being recognised that the parity and time at which each of the countries now off gold could undertake to stabilise must be decided by the respective governments concerned.

II. The signatory governments whose currencies are on the gold standard re-assert that it is their determination to maintain the free working of that standard at the existing gold parities within the framework of their respective monetary laws.

III. The signatory governments whose currencies are not on the gold standard, without in any way prejudicing their own future ratios to gold, take note of the above declaration and recognise its importance. They re-affirm as indicated in Paragraph I above that the ultimate objective of their monetary policy is to restore, under proper conditions, an international monetary standard based on gold.

IV. Each of the signatory governments whose currencies are not on the gold standard undertakes to adopt the measures which it may deem most appropriate to limit exchange speculation, and each of the other signatory governments undertakes to co-operate to the same end.

V. Each of the undersigned governments agrees to ask its central bank to co-operate with the central banks of the other signatory governments, in limiting speculation in the exchanges and, when the time comes, in re-establishing a general international gold standard.

VI. The present declaration is open to signature by other governments whether their currencies are on the gold standard or not.

This joint declaration was intended to serve the following purposes: (1) to remove the prevailing uncertainty as to whether or not an international gold standard will be re-established; (2) to strengthen the position of the gold countries with respect to speculative activities directed against their currencies, by the psychological effect of their strong declaration of policy and by the announcement on the part of the non-gold countries, implied in their recognition of the importance of this declaration of policy, that they would not make any attempts to force the gold countries into a devaluation of their currencies or to prevail upon them to do so voluntarily; and (3) to diminish the general instability of foreign exchanges by concerted action against speculative activity. As a first step this clearly would involve a decision to control at least temporarily the foreign exchange fluctuations of the two major currencies—the dollar and the pound sterling.

According to reports which were current at the time, this text of the joint declaration was acceptable to the American delegation, as well as to Professor Raymond Moley, at that time assistant secretary of state, who was in London on a brief visit and took part in the consultations. In any event, however, formal acceptance on the part of the United States was conditional on the President's approval. The proposed text was submitted to the President on June 30. It was emphatically rejected by him in a message, which he addressed to the conference on July 3, and which read as follows:

I would regard it as a catastrophe amounting to a world tragedy if the great conference of nations, called to bring about a more real and permanent financial stability and a greater prosperity to the masses of all nations, should, in advance of any serious effort to consider these broader problems, allow itself to be diverted by the proposal of a purely artificial and temporary experiment affecting the monetary exchange of a few nations only. Such action, such diversion, shows a singular lack of proportion and a failure to remember the larger purposes for which the Economic Conference originally was called together.

I do not relish the thought that insistence on such action should be made an excuse for the continuance of the basic economic errors that underlie so much of the present world-wide depression.

The world will not long be lulled by the specious fallacy of achieving a temporary and probably an artificial stability in foreign exchange on the part of a few large countries only.

The sound internal economic system of a nation is a greater factor in its well-being than the price of its currency in changing terms of the currencies of other nations.

It is for this reason that reduced cost of government, adequate government income, and ability to service government debts are all so important to ultimate stability. So, too, old fetishes of so-called international bankers are being replaced by efforts to plan national currencies with the objective of giving to those currencies a continuing purchasing power which does not greatly vary in terms of the commodities and need of modern civilization. Let me be frank in saying that the United States seeks the kind of dollar which a generation hence will have the same purchasing and debt-paying power as the dollar value we hope to attain in the near future. That objective means more to the good of other nations than a fixed ratio for a month or two in terms of the pound or franc.

Our broad purpose is the permanent stabilisation of every nation's currency. Gold or gold and silver can well continue to be a metallic reserve behind currencies, but this is not the time to dissipate gold reserves. When the world works out concerted policies in the majority of nations to produce balanced budgets and living within their means then we can properly discuss a better distribution of the world's gold and silver supply to act as a reserve base of national currencies.

Restoration of world trade is an important partner both in the means and in the result. Here also temporary exchange fixing is not the true answer. We must rather mitigate existing embargoes to make easier the exchange of products which one nation has and the other nation has not.

The conference was called to better and perhaps to cure fundamental economic ills. It must not be diverted from that effort.

President Roosevelt's message changed the whole character of the London discussions. It introduced a new issue of vital significance. In the fifth paragraph of his message, the President enunciated his advocacy of a monetary organization based on a stable commodity price level, rather than on stability of foreign exchanges. Up to this time the second sub-commission of the Monetary and Financial Commission, which had this topic under consideration, had been conducting its work on the basis of a draft resolution, introduced on June 19 by Senator Pittman, in the name of the American delegation, which began as follows:

Whereas confusion now exists in the field of international exchange, and

Whereas it is essential to world recovery that an international monetary standard should be re-established,

Now, THEREFORE, BE IT RESOLVED that all the nations participating in this conference agree

a) That it is in the interests of all concerned that stability in the international monetary field be attained as quickly as practicable;

b) That gold should be re-established as the international measure of exchange values. . . .

The new American position was made even clearer in a second message to the conference, transmitted by the American delegation on July 5, where it was presented as follows:

The revaluation of the dollar in terms of American commodities is an end from which the government and the people of the United States cannot be diverted. We wish to make this perfectly clear: we are interested in American commodity prices. What is to be the value of the dollar in terms of foreign currencies is not and cannot be our immediate concern. The exchange value of the dollar will ultimately depend upon the success of other nations in raising the prices of their own commodities in terms of their national moneys and cannot be determined in advance of our knowledge of such fact. There is nothing in our policy inimical to the interest of any other country and we are confident that no other country would seek to embarrass us in the attainment of economic ends required for our economic health.

The conference was asked by the American delegation to continue with its task by discussing the numerous other problems before it. It was stated that the American government found it "difficult to conceive that the view which it has been our obvious duty to take on the minor issue of temporary stabilization can in any way diminish the advisability of such discussion."

IV. THE IMPASSE

The American request that the conference proceed with its work was in response to the demand (which began to be made by a number of delegations as soon as the President's message was received) that the conference should adjourn forthwith. A large number of delegations took the position that a *de facto* stabilization of foreign exchanges, as a determinant of future policy in this field, was to them not a "minor issue," as it appeared to the American government, but a decidedly major one —in fact, the crux of the whole situation. They reiterated their view that no commitments in the field of commercial policy or of foreign exchange controls were possible until it was known at least approximately what the values of national currency units would be. Moreover, since no country represented in London was prepared to follow the United States in a policy which had for its objective a rapid and very large rise in commodity prices, to be followed by an experiment with monetary organization based on a stabilization of national price levels as distinguished from foreign exchange stability; and since the government of the United States formally announced its determination not to be diverted from such a policy, a number of important delegations expressed their conviction that a basis for agreement no longer existed and that any further discussion at the conference would be useless.

The question whether or not the conference should be adjourned came up for decision by the bureau, or steering committee, of the parley. In the sharp debate which took place, Secretary Hull, the head of the American delegation, argued for a continuation of the conference and a further exploration of the numerous topics on its agenda other than the foreign exchange question. The representatives of the gold countries urged immediate adjournment. When the matter was finally put to a vote, the representatives of the other non-gold countries joined with the United States for strategic reasons, and the London session was saved from immediate dissolution by a majority of one.

But the usefulness of the conference, so far as the work of its London session was concerned, was definitely at an end. Even with the controversy over the foreign exchanges out of the way, the task of the conference might have been too difficult to yield any substantial results. In the course of its discussions, the thorny problem of commercial policy was barely touched upon, and it was not at all impossible that the whole London effort might have broken down on that vital issue. But with the controversy over foreign exchanges as sharp as it became after President Roosevelt's message, the conference could not possibly avoid a hopeless impasse.

V. RESULTS AND REPORTS OF THE CONFERENCE

The London session continued for nearly three weeks after the decision of the bureau, and then went into indefinite recess, the interval being spent in half-hearted discussion of a number of problems and in the preparation of reports by the various commissions and sub-commissions. These reports, which were presented to the last plenary meeting of the London session on July 27, recorded the results of seven weeks of discussion. They are given in full in the Documentary Appendix (see pages 167-78).

The sub-commission on immediate measures for financial reconstruction reported its failure to arrive at any agreement on the question of credit policy and price levels, already noted on page 76 above. It further announced the unanimous adoption by its members of a resolution on private indebtedness. With respect to the other items on its agenda, it stated that "the discussion did not proceed far enough to do more than outline the main problems to be solved."

The sub-commission on permanent measures for the re-establishment of an international monetary standard dealt with questions for which no immediate action was required, with the sole exception of the silver problem. As a result, it was able to reach agreement on most items of its agenda and to adopt a number of resolutions, based, in large part, on the draft resolution presented by

Senator Pittman, which was referred to on page 84 above and the full text of which is given in the Documentary Appendix (pp. 159-60). The principal recommendations of the sub-commission may be summarized as follows:

It is important and "in the interests of everyone concerned that stability in the international monetary field be attained as quickly as practicable." Such stability should be based on the re-establishment of gold "as the international measure of exchange value," each nation reserving full right to choose the time for returning to the gold standard and the metal content of its basic currency unit. In the restored gold standard system, gold should not be used for internal circulation in the form of coins or certificates, but should serve as a central bank reserve and as a means for settling international payments. In the countries in which the system of percentage gold cover is used, the minimum ratio should not be higher than 25 per cent, instead of one-third to two-fifths as has been customary hitherto. The purpose of this would be to afford the gold standard greater elasticity, but the reduction of the reserve ratios "must not be taken as an excuse for unduly building up a large superstructure of notes and credit." In other words, "the effect of this resolution should be to increase the free reserve of central banks and thereby to strengthen their position," rather than to provide the basis for an undue expansion of currency and credit. Further, independent central banks should be created "in such developed countries as have not at present an adequate central banking institution," and close and continuous co-operation between central banks should be developed, with the Bank for International Settlements serving "to improve contact" and "as an instrument for common action."

The resolution on silver followed Senator Pittman's draft in recommending that an agreement should be reached between the principal silver-producing countries and the countries which are holders of large stocks of that metal for the purpose of mitigating fluctuations in the price of silver, and that all nations should refrain from debasing any future issues of silver coins below a fineness of 800/1000. It does not contain Senator Pittman's proposal that all existing subsidiary coins (which in many countries have, since the war, been reduced to a fineness of 500/1000) be remonetized to a fineness of at least 800, nor his recommendation that the metal cover of central banks should, in the future, consist of gold to the extent of 80 per cent and of silver to the extent of 20 per cent. On the other hand, it contains an added recommendation that silver coins should be substituted for notes of smaller denominations. A formal agreement embodying some of these recommendations was actually negotiated and signed during the conference.

Finally, the sub-commission worked out and adopted a statement of general principles on central banking policy, which was to serve as a sort of manual of rules for the gold standard game. This statement was adopted by all nations, except the United States, the Federal Reserve Board in this country taking the position that it would be premature for it to accept any such commitments in advance of an official decision by the United States government to return to a free international gold standard, for which the statement of principles was to be a part of the foundation.[4]

The question of foreign exchange stability, while discussed directly only in the Monetary and Financial Com-

[4] The full text of this statement is given in Appendix E, pp. 176-77.

mision, dominated also all the discussion in the sphere of economic policies and was reflected especially in the final report of the sub-commission on commercial policy. In the general observations, with which the sub-commission prefaced its report, it was stated:

It should be stressed at the outset that the hypothesis on which the whole work of the sub-commission was based was the stabilization, or at any rate the *de facto* stability, of currencies. When events showed that this hypothesis could not be realized, at any rate at the moment, several countries, in view of the fluctuations in the exchanges, deemed it necessary to reserve full liberty of action in the matter either of quantitative restrictions, or foreign exchange control, or customs tariffs. Other delegations were of opinion that it would be expedient to endeavor to draw up a positive and constructive program, indicating the measures which they were prepared to take in the sphere of commercial policy when stability has been achieved. This divergence of opinion made unanimous agreement impossible.

Accordingly, the sub-commission's report on this vital issue consisted merely of a listing of the topics discussed and the various proposals made with respect to them by individual countries. For the rest, the reports of the economic sub-commission dealt with such questions as international producers' agreements, subsidies of various sorts, veterinary controls, and other similar measures of indirect protectionism. On none of these questions was definite agreement recorded in the reports.

After the adoption of these reports, the conference adjourned, subject to call by its bureau, which was constituted into a permanent and continuing organ. The bureau, in turn, set up an executive committee consisting of the president and vice-president of the conference, and of the presidents, vice-presidents, and *rapporteurs* of the main commissions. There was a proviso that

each of these members of the committee might be replaced by another person nominated by his respective
government. Taking into account the nationalities of its
members, the executive committee thus consists, in effect,
of representatives of the following countries: The
United States, Great Britain, France, Germany, Italy,
Holland, Austria, and Argentina. This executive committee is charged with the task of preparing any future
session of the conference—if and when the parley should
be reconvened.

Whether or not the conference will be resumed will
depend upon the possibility of finding a common ground
and a basis of agreement among the principal nations of
the world. And monetary policy is the principal domain
in which such common ground would have to be found.

CHAPTER V

MONETARY POSITION SINCE THE LONDON CONFERENCE

While the London session of the World Monetary and Economic Conference failed to solve the monetary problem, or even to bring it nearer solution, it served to throw the basic monetary issues into sharper relief than ever before. At the close of that session, the world monetary position was different in three important respects from what it had been seven weeks previously, when the conference began. The countries still on the gold standard became strengthened in their determination to retain their existing monetary organization and banded themselves into a monetary alliance, known as the Gold Bloc, for the purpose of carrying out this decision. The members of the British Commonwealth of Nations, which had had a loose monetary association since they had abandoned the gold standard, took important steps toward converting this association into a more formal alliance. Finally, public policy in the United States became directed, for an unpredictable period ahead, toward a still greater subordination of international to national factors, which, in the monetary sphere, found expression in continued instability of the dollar exchange rate.

The attitudes of these three groups of countries constitute the essential elements in the monetary position of the world today. The principal developments which have occurred since the end of the London session are described in this chapter.

I. THE GOLD BLOC

The Gold Bloc grew out of President Roosevelt's rejection of the draft joint declaration quoted on page 81. A few hours after the President's message reached the conference, the representatives of the six countries still on the full gold standard—France, Italy, Belgium, Holland, Switzerland, and Poland—issued the following statement:

The undersigned governments, convinced that the maintenance of their currencies is essential for the economic and financial recovery of the world and of credit and for the safeguarding of social progress in their respective countries, confirm their intention to maintain the free functioning of the gold standard in their respective countries at the existing gold parities and within the framework of existing monetary laws. They ask their central banks to keep in close touch to give the maximum efficacy to this declaration.

Five days later, on July 8, the heads of the six central banks met in Paris and agreed on a procedure to be followed in giving effect to the London declaration of their governments. The arrangements perfected at this meeting were designed to combat speculation in the currencies of the six gold standard countries, both within and outside their respective frontiers. They involved no new and startling innovations, but consisted mainly of an agreement for closely co-ordinated action, to be put into effect immediately.

The London declaration and the Paris meeting had an immediate steadying influence on monetary conditions in the gold countries. Their exchange rates, which, during the preceding weeks, had been falling on frequent occasions below the gold export points and causing outward gold movements, rose swiftly above the gold import points, and gold began to flow back into their reserves. By the beginning of August, each one of these countries showed a marked improvement in the condition of its gold stocks. The incipient panic, which seemed to be looming just ahead in all six of the gold countries as a result of a heavy drain from the reserves of Holland and Switzerland, was over—at least for the time being.

The general position of the gold group was announced to the conference by its acknowledged spokesman in London, M. Georges Bonnet, the French minister of finance. The action of the new bloc, M. Bonnet explained, is inspired "neither by ill-will nor by a desire to criticise." The six countries are acting, first of all, in what they believe to be their own best interests. They are, however, convinced that what they do would also serve the cause of all nations. For,

If, against the will of states and the express determination of their governments, the stable currencies of European countries were suddenly subjected to blind forces of speculation, this would introduce into the troubled world a new element of uncertainty which could only complicate matters.

The gold countries feel certain that sooner or later stability will be re-established in the international monetary field through a universal restoration of the gold standard. Their continued adherence to that standard has, in their view, three advantages: (1) It safeguards them from what they believe the inevitable evils of currency instability; (2) it maintains stable foreign exchanges based on gold throughout the area represented by their group of countries; and (3) it constitutes an important nucleus for the eventual resoration of an international gold standard.

The arrangements set up by these countries in July

continue in operation today. They will obviously remain effective only so long as the basic monetary policy within each of the six countries remains as announced in their London declaration of July 3. This policy has widespread domestic support within the four countries of the group which have gone through a period of fiscal disorders, fluctuating foreign exchanges, and final depreciation of their currency units. In the other two countries— Holland and Switzerland—the gold content of whose currencies is still what it was before the war—there are strong movements in favor of depreciation for the sake of foreign trade advantage or an adjustment of internal debt relations. These movements have not, however, as yet proved to be sufficiently strong to influence official policy.

With respect to commodity prices, the authorities in these countries continue to hold the view announced by their representatives at the London Conference. They still maintain that a rise in prices, as an antecedent to economic recovery, induced by such monetary means as the depreciation of the currency and fiscal inflation, is bound to do more harm than good.

While these countries have made clear their determination to maintain the gold standard, their ability to do so depends upon a number of factors, domestic as well as international. They have so far demonstrated a capacity for defending their currencies from international speculation. Two principal dangers confront them: (1) a possibility of an extensive flight of capital, induced mainly by internal political and fiscal developments; and (2) a continuation and increase of monetary uncertainty in other parts of the world, especially in Great Britain and the United States.

II. BRITISH IMPERIAL MONETARY ALLIANCE

The arrangement made by the members of the British Commonwealth of Nations was embodied in a formal declaration signed by the representatives of Great Britain, Canada, India, Australia, New Zealand, and the Union of South Africa, on July 27, that is, on the last day of the London session. In this declaration, the six countries re-affirmed the monetary resolutions adopted by them at the Ottawa Conference in the summer of 1932 and reinforced the position taken there by a number of new decisions.

The basic view set forth in the London declaration was substantially the same as that expounded at the conference by the British Chancellor of the Exchequer and summarized on page 79 above. On the question of monetary organization the declaration read as follows:

> The ultimate aim of monetary policy should be the restoration of a satisfactory international gold standard under which international co-operation would be secured and maintained with a view to avoiding, so far as may be found practicable, undue fluctuations in the purchasing power of gold. The problem with which the world is faced is to reconcile the stability of exchange rates with a reasonable measure of stability, not merely in a price level of a particular country, but in world prices. Effective action in this matter must largely depend on international co-operation, and in any further sessions of the World Monetary and Economic Conference this subject must have special prominence.

This statement of policy is far from being precise and definite. In fact, on the whole vital issue of monetary organization there is very little precision in the London declaration—beyond the official acceptance by the six countries of the restoration of an international gold standard as an ultimate aim of their monetary policy and their expressed willingness to negotiate with other nations as to the conditions for re-establishment and future maintenance of such a standard.

A rise in the general level of commodity prices is still put forward as the principal condition precedent to a return to gold, but what is meant by this is stated in the following vague terms:

> Any price level would be satisfactory which restores the normal activity of industry and employment, which ensures an economic return to the producer of primary commodities, and which harmonizes the burden of debts and fixed charges with economic capacity. It is important that the rise in prices should not be carried to such a pitch as to produce an inflated scale of profits and threaten a disturbance of equilibrium in the opposite direction.

Equally lacking in precision is the statement with regard to the need of reconciling stability of exchanges with stability of prices. Both the definition of the kind and degree of stability that are desired and the devising of machinery for assuring such stability are expressly left to future international negotiations and agreement.

Somewhat more precise are the arrangements for the immediate future. Pending international agreement along the lines just indicated, the six signatories solemnly announced that they "recognize the importance of stability of exchange rates between the countries of the Empire in the interests of trade," and that "this objective will be constantly kept in mind in determining their monetary policy." They reiterated the determination of their countries to promote a rise in commodity prices, but stated that action would have to be based on a common policy, if stable exchanges are to be maintained. With a view to making such a policy effective, they undertook to recommend to their governments the need of consulting "with one another from time to time on monetary and economic policy with a view to establishing their common purpose and to the framing of such measures as may conduce towards its achievement."

It was emphasized that the exchange stabilization action is not to be in terms of gold or of gold currencies. It is to be a purely intra-Imperial affair. The machinery proposed is designed merely to keep the Imperial currencies stable in terms of the pound sterling, the latter being free to move up or down with respect to any other currencies. But while the Dominion currencies are thus to follow faithfully the course of the sterling exchange, Great Britain has undertaken to consult with her partners in the arrangement before taking any decisive steps in modifying or fixing the exchange rate of the pound.

Other non-gold countries were invited to join in this arrangement. The invitation was addressed to countries having close trade relations with the British Empire, that is, to the Scandinavian and certain South American countries. This, it was urged, "would make possible the attainment and maintenance of exchange stability over a still wider area."

The British Commonwealth of Nations continues today to operate, in its monetary policy, on the basis of the London arrangement. It is admittedly a makeshift and temporary policy. In the field of foreign exchanges, the arrangement is designed to leave the hands of the Imperial Monetary Alliance, sometimes called by the rather bizarre name of "sterlingarea," free with respect to the future course of the dollar exchange. Under it, Great Britain and her Imperial partners remain unhampered if they should decide to counter any further depreciation of the dollar by a depreciation of their currencies. This deferment of decision with regard to a definitive stabilization of the exchange is of special importance to such British Dominions as Canada and Australia, which find themselves in a competitive position with respect to the United States as exporters of a number of important agricultural staples. Provision with regard to it was written into the London declaration principally at their insistence.

But the continued maintenance of currencies unanchored to gold is regarded mainly as a trade adjustment mechanism, rather than as a price-raising device. As their representatives at the London Conference made clear, Great Britain and her partners place principal reliance, on the monetary side, upon cheap and plentiful credit as an instrument for raising commodity prices. Their authorities are strongly insistent upon the need of balanced budgets, and are vigorously opposed to any form of fiscal inflation. For the future, they are now definitely committed to a policy of favoring the reestablishment of an international gold standard—if and when decision in the United States and international agreement on what they regard as indispensable conditions render the restoration of an international monetary standard feasible.

III. DEVELOPMENTS IN THE UNITED STATES

For three months following the London Conference the official monetary policy in the United States remained substantially as laid down in the President's message to the conference. The primary objective, as stated in the message dated July 5, was as follows: "The first task is to restore prices to a level at which industry and, above all, agriculture, can function profitably and efficiently. The second task is to preserve the stability of this adjustment once achieved."

In the process of inducing the price rise only a part of the machinery devised for this purpose at the last session of Congress was utilized by the President between July and late October. Principal reliance was placed on the mechanisms provided by the Agricultural Adjustment Act and the National Industrial Recovery Act, including the program of public works. Large open market purchases of government securities were made by the Federal Reserve system, but on its own initiative rather than that of the Treasury. Neither the issue of greenbacks, the direct sale of Treasury obligations to Federal Reserve Banks, nor a definitive devaluation of the dollar was resorted to.

With respect to the foreign exchange value of the dollar, the position remained as announced in London—namely, that "what is to be the value of the dollar in terms of foreign currencies is not and cannot be our immediate concern." Accordingly, the foreign exchange policy pursued was passive in character. The exchange rate of the dollar was not deliberately depressed, but was simply permitted to fluctuate more or less freely of its own accord. An absence of definite commitments for the future—as to what is to be the permanent value of the dollar and, indeed, as to the future character of the whole monetary system—was relied upon to keep the dollar exchange rate moving in a generally downward, rather than upward, direction.

The middle of July marked the peak of the general price rise since the upward movement began last spring. In the second half of that month, there was a sharp recession, followed, after some fluctuations, by a new upturn in September. Then came another recession, which continued into October. (See the chart on page 118.) Under the influence of these vagaries in the price movements, three important viewpoints developed in the country.

According to the first of these viewpoints, the principal reason for the price recession and the subsequent failure of the price indexes to re-attain and surpass the July level lay in inadequate vigor of monetary policy. Since the prices which had sustained the greatest relative loss were those of primary agricultural products, the pressure for more monetary action came primarily from the agricultural interests and their political spokesmen. The instrument of action pressed by the advocates of this view was the expansion of currency through the issue of greenbacks, authorized by the Thomas amendment.

The second viewpoint found its principal expression in the renewed energy exhibited by those who favored devaluation of the dollar as a means of price stimulation. The value of the paper dollar, as measured in gold through the foreign exchanges, showed a rising tendency after the middle of September and especially during the first half of October. Since continuing exchange depreciation was regarded by this group as an indispensable condition for rising commodity prices, the improvement in the exchange rate was viewed by them with genuine alarm. Hence they urged upon the President the adoption of an active policy of dollar depreciation.

The method proposed for the immediate future did not involve a definite reduction in the weight of the dollar, that is, a re-definition of the dollar in terms of its gold content. Nor did it contemplate the creation of machinery for direct foreign exchange control. The plan called rather for the establishment of government monopoly for the purchase of gold newly mined in the United States. Two alternative procedures were presented for the President's consideration: (1) To set the price of gold immediately at $41.34 an ounce, which would represent a 50 per cent reduction in the weight of the gold dollar—the maximum authorized under the Thomas amendment; or (2) to begin purchases of gold at a price corresponding closely to the prevailing rate of foreign exchange and gradually to raise it toward the maximum authorized figures. In the former case, it was maintained, American commodity prices would almost immediately rise to something like the pre-depression level; in the latter case the rise would occur by gradual stages unaffected by speculative or other factors in the international exchange market. In other words, this policy was intended to give us independent control of the American commodity price level.[1]

Finally, there was a third clearly defined viewpoint in accordance with which the failure of prices to respond to the measures of stimulation which were being put into effect was principally the result of hesitation on the part of business enterprise to go forward in the face of the existing uncertainty as to monetary policies. This, it was pointed out, was especially the case in connection with business transactions involving time contracts. Of particular importance, it was argued, was the difficulty in floating bond issues for the financing of normal capital outlays. Accordingly, the adherents of this view urged upon the President the need of re-establishing stable monetary conditions by enunciating a definite policy with respect to the permanent gold content of the dollar.

[1] The theory underlying this argument will be discussed in the next chapter.

The President's decision was announced in a radio address delivered on October 22. His pronouncement was hastened by the rapid development of discontent in the farming districts of the Middle West. At the same time many of the President's advisers appeared to have been greatly perturbed over the possible effects upon the economic and monetary position of the United States of such European political developments as Germany's withdrawal from the League of Nations and the Cabinet crisis in France. It was felt that events in Europe might cause a substantial repatriation of American funds held abroad, causing an upward movement in the dollar exchange rate, and thus reacting unfavorably on the course of commodity prices in this country.

In his radio address the President reiterated that it was the definite policy of the government to raise commodity prices. He announced himself as being far from satisfied with the rise that had taken place thus far, especially as relating to the prices of some agricultural commodities. But, at the same time, in replying to those who advocate greenback inflation, he warned against too great impatience in the handling of so complex a problem and pointed out that, in spite of the recession in agricultural prices from the speculative levels reached in July, the average of agricultural prices in October was still substantially higher than it had been in the spring.

Replying, on the other hand, to those who urged permanent stabilization by means of a definitive fixation of the weight of the gold dollar, the President stated bluntly that the advocates of this course of action "are putting the cart before the horse." He said:

It is the government's policy to restore the price level first. I would not know, and no one else could tell, just what the permanent valuation of the dollar will be. To guess at a permanent gold valuation now would certainly require later changes caused by later facts.

The following objectives of the price-raising policy were laid down:

The object has been the attainment of such a level as will enable agriculture and industry once more to give work to the unemployed.

It has been to make possible the payment of public and private debts more nearly at the price level at which they were incurred.

It has been gradually to restore a balance in the price structure so that farmers may exchange their products for the products of industry on a fairer exchange basis.

It has been and is also the purpose to prevent prices from rising beyond the point necessary to attain these ends.

The President pointed out that the attainment of these objectives might prove to be a slower process than is desired by some groups "because hundreds of different kinds of crops and industrial occupations in the huge territory that makes up this nation are involved, we cannot reach the goal in only a few months. We may take one year or two years or three." He was, however, equally emphatic in stating that "it is definitely a part of our policy to increase the rise and to extend it to those products which have as yet felt no benefit. If we cannot do this way we will do it another. Do it we will."

The President accepted the plan of raising prices through direct depreciation of the paper dollar in terms of gold, and endorsed the idea that the control of American prices must be freed from international influences. His pronouncement read as follows:

Because of conditions in this country and because of events beyond our control in other parts of the world, it becomes increasingly important to develop and apply the further measures which may be necessary from time to time to control the gold value of our own dollar at home.

Our dollar is now altogether too greatly influenced by the accidents of international trade, by the internal policies of other nations, and by political disturbances in other continents.

Therefore the United States must take firmly into its own hands the control of the gold value of our dollar. This is necessary in order to prevent dollar disturbances from swinging us away from our ultimate goal, namely, the continued recovery of our commodity prices.

As a further effective means to this end, I am going to establish a government market for gold in the United States. Therefore, under the clearly defined authority of existing law, I am authorizing the Reconstruction Finance Corporation to buy gold newly mined in the United States at prices to be determined from time to time after consultation with the Secretary of the Treasury and the President. Whenever necessary to the end in view, we shall also buy or sell gold in the world market.

Finally, the President re-asserted that after the desired price level had been restored, the permanent policy would be to maintain that level. "When we have restored the price level, we shall seek to establish and maintain a dollar which will not change its purchasing and debt-paying power during the succeeding generation. I said that in my message to the American delegation in London last July. And I say it now once more."

After describing the machinery of a government market for gold, he said:

My aim in taking this step is to establish and maintain continuous control.

This is a policy and not an expedient.

It is not to be used merely to offset a temporary fall in prices. We are thus continuing to move toward a managed currency.

This gold purchase plan was put into operation on October 25. For the first few days, the operations were confined to domestic purchases of newly mined gold at official prices set at progressively higher levels. On October 30, decision was announced to extend the operations to foreign markets as well, and arrangements began to be perfected for the purchase of gold abroad. An analysis of the theoretical validity of the plan, of its possible efficacy, and of some of its general economic effects will be given in the two concluding chapters.

CHAPTER VI

THE GOLD PURCHASE PLAN

The American policy embarked upon in late October embodies a new device for attempting to raise commodity prices in this country by monetary action. The United States government has thus definitely assumed a role of leadership in applying the theory that rising prices induced by monetary policies are a prerequisite to economic recovery. This policy involves, not concerted international action of the sort so frequently discussed at Geneva and London, but independent action by a single country directed toward management of its domestic commodity price level. In view of the vital economic importance of the issues involved, it is necessary to analyze in some detail this new development of American policy.

I. THEORETICAL BASIS OF THE PLAN

The basic theory which apparently underlies the new policy is, stated in its simplest terms, that the price level is directly related to the *value* of gold.[1] Gold is regarded as a world commodity, and its value in terms of goods is, therefore, determined by world supply in relation to world demand. Hence the value of gold, or the amount of goods which exchanges for a given weight of gold, tends to be the same in every country. If the supply of gold increases faster than the demand for gold, its value

[1] No explicit statement has been made by the government as to the precise theory on which it is operating. But the principles involved are reasonably clear from the procedure that is being followed.

will fall, and this means (assuming no change in the commodity situation) that each ounce of gold will then exchange for a smaller quantity of other goods than before. Putting the matter another way, more gold would have to be offered for the same quantity of commodities, and the price level would rise everywhere.

A. The Price of Gold and the Price of Commodities

Each country has its own monetary unit, in terms of which all commodities are said to have a price. In the United States, the dollar is the unit, and the price of any article is the number of dollars for which it will exchange. However, the definition of a dollar differs in accordance with whether or not a country is on the gold standard.

Since 1834 the dollar has contained 23.22 grains of pure gold.[2] At this rate, an ounce of gold would divide into 20.67 dollar units. Since any individual bringing an ounce of gold to the mint could always obtain for it $20.67 in currency,[3] the price of an ounce of gold was said to be $20.67. Paper dollars and all other forms of currency were freely redeemable in gold at the legally defined ratio of 23.22 grains per dollar. Accordingly any person in possession of gold could always convert it into currency at the rate of $20.67 per ounce, and any person wishing to obtain gold could always purchase it at the same rate. The price of gold, therefore, remained fixed at $20.67 an ounce.

With the suspension of the gold standard, it is no longer possible to exchange paper money for gold at the fixed rate. When this happens it usually becomes

---

[2] With alloy added the full weight was 25.8 grains.
[3] Less a slight charge to cover minting expenses.

necessary to offer more paper money for a given weight of gold. This may be said to mean either that the price of gold has risen or that the paper dollar has depreciated. If for example the paper currency depreciates by 20 per cent, the price of gold would rise to $25.80 an ounce instead of remaining at $20.67.

So long as the price of gold remains fixed, changes in the commodity price level in any country, according to the theory back of the gold purchase plan, result *solely* from changes in the value of gold. However, if the price of gold ceases to be fixed, changes in the price level are the result of two factors; the value of gold in terms of commodities, and the price of gold in terms of the national monetary unit. The assumed relationship between changes in the price of gold and changes in the commodity price level may be illustrated as follows: Suppose an ounce of gold, when its price is $20.00, would exchange for ten units of commodities. The average price of each commodity unit would be $2.00. Now suppose as a result of the depreciation the price of gold rises to $30.00 an ounce. The average price of the commodities in question would then automatically become $3.00.[4]

From this relationship, the adherents of the theory deduce the governing principle that a national price level can be *consciously regulated* by manipulating the price of gold. This, it is maintained, can be done by legally altering the weight of the gold dollar, so long as the United States is redeeming its paper currency in gold, or, in the absence of redemption, by offering a larger

[4] This, according to the theory, would be precisely true only if the world value of gold in terms of commodities meanwhile remained unchanged. If the value of gold, as distinguished from its price, were at the same time falling, the advance in commodity prices would be proportionally increased, or vice versa.

or a smaller number of paper dollars for an ounce of gold. Thus gold is regarded as the key to commodity prices whether the country is on or off the gold standard.

B. The Price-Raising Mechanism

The new plan is expected to operate upon the principle of regulating the commodity price level by controlling the price of gold. Since the country is off the gold standard, the American price level is to be raised by a progressive depreciation of the paper dollar in terms of gold, that is, by offering more and more paper for gold. In effect, the same result is expected to be attained that would be reached by a series of legal reductions in the weight of the gold dollar, which would automatically raise the dollar price of gold. The gold purchase plan is held to have an advantage in that it permits continuous manipulation of the price of gold and the adjustment of its value in the light of changing conditions. It is also regarded as opening the way to a permanent system of controlling prices through currency manipulation.

In devising the machinery for this purpose, an important difficulty had to be surmounted. At a result of the anti-hoarding order of April 5, it became impossible to buy or sell gold freely within the country. In the absence of a domestic gold market, no means existed for either registering or influencing the price of gold in terms of paper dollars. However, gold could still be bought and sold internationally through the foreign exchange process, and the foreign exchange quotations in terms of other currencies became in fact the sole means of measuring the price of gold in paper dollars. For example, before the suspension of the gold standard by the United

States, the amount of gold in the dollar was 25.5 times the amount of gold in the French franc. The dollar was, therefore, worth 25.5 francs, and, when exchange was at par, was quoted at that rate in the foreign exchange markets. After the suspension of the gold standard, the dollar gradually declined in relation to the gold franc. It was quoted on November 1, 1933 as the equivalent of only 16.8 francs. Since the French franc still represented the same amount of gold as before, the foreign exchanges registered a depreciation of 35 per cent in the dollar.

This depreciation of the dollar in terms of foreign exchange was giving us a rising price of gold. However, as previously indicated, it was subject to general factors, speculative and otherwise, influencing the foreign exchange rate, and showed substantial fluctuations. This, it was argued, was the result of the fact that the government was pursuing a passive policy with reference to foreign exchange. A continuous rise in the price of gold, it was held, could be obtained only by inaugurating an active policy of controlled depreciation. Accordingly, as we have seen, a government monopoly was set up for the purchase of all gold newly mined in the United States. Under this arrangement, the Reconstruction Finance Corporation, acting as the government agency for the purpose, would offer arbitrarily determined amounts of paper money for each ounce of gold brought to it.

Since, according to the theory, the American price level can be uninterruptedly raised only by a sustained rise in the price of gold, and since for this purpose a progressive depreciation of the dollar on the foreign exchanges is indispensable, the success of the plan de-

pended fundamentally upon the effects of gold purchases upon the exchanges. It was apparently thought
that the mere raising of the price of gold by the government through gold purchases in the United States

Daily Official Price of Gold Compared with Daily Quotations of the French Franc[a]

(In terms of the dollar. $20.67 per ounce = 100 for the price of gold; par of exchange = 100 for the exchange quotation.)

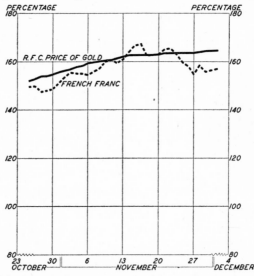

[a] Official price as set by Reconstruction Finance Corporation; exchange
quotations based on cable rates.

would automatically depreciate the dollar in foreign
exchange quotations. It was recognized, however, that
this might not prove to be the case; hence it was announced that the government would be prepared to buy
and sell gold in foreign markets, thereby directly influencing foreign exchange quotations.

Another consequence expected from the operation of

the plan is a stimulation of gold mining. This, according to the theory, would serve to expand the total world supply of gold in relation to other commodities, lower the value of gold, and thus provide an added impetus for an upward movement of the price level in all countries.

The movements of the foreign exchange value of the dollar in relation to the price of gold set by the United States government are shown on the accompanying chart. It will be seen that no close correspondence is revealed. The dollar in the exchange markets has been at times above and at other times well below the Reconstruction Finance Corporation price for newly mined gold, and it is evident that speculative sentiment has continued to be the controlling influence. No official information concerning the precise amount of gold purchased abroad has been made available. The effects of changes in the price of gold upon commodity prices are discussed in later sections of this chapter.

C. The Price-Stabilization Mechanism

In addition to this mechanism for *raising* the price level, the new plan forecasts, as noted in the preceding chapter, the policy to be pursued after the price level has reached the desired height. In announcing that the machinery for regulating the price of gold is intended "to establish and maintain continuous control," and that "this is a policy and not an expedient," representing a step "toward a managed currency," the President indicated that the currency management is to be of the "compensated dollar" type, rather than of the type described on pages 18-21 above, which would be based on central control and conscious manipulation of the volume of currency and credit.

The purpose of the compensated dollar scheme is to prevent fluctuations in the American commodity price level after the desired level of prices has once been attained. If the price level should show a rise in a given period—as a result of whatever causes—the weight of gold in the dollar would be increased by the same percentage, thereby restoring the previous level of prices. Similarly, if prices should fall, the gold weight of the dollar would be diminished sufficiently to restore the former level. In other words, the effects of changes in the value of gold would be counteracted by arbitrary changes in the price of gold. If gold is not to be utilized as a medium of exchange, it would not in practice be necessary to coin gold at the varying weights established from time to time. Under such conditions, it is held, all that would be needed would be simply to announce the official price of gold and to establish machinery for government purchase and sale of gold at this official price.

By such a system of monetary management, it is believed, the American price level can not only be raised to the level obtaining prior to the depression, but can also henceforth be completely stabilized. It can be made entirely independent of changes in the world value of gold, of fluctuations in the output of new gold, of shifts in the foreign exchange value of the dollar, and of movements of commodity prices in other countries. It is contended by the leading advocates of the theory that the effects of changes in the price of gold upon commodity prices would be *mathematically precise*. They state, for example, that "if prices rise 0.1 per cent in a week, the weight of gold purchasable by a dollar would be increased 0.1 per cent until any rise was corrected." Conversely, "if prices fell 0.1 per cent, the weight of the gold purchasable by a dollar would be decreased 0.1 per cent."[5]

Such are the basic principles on which the gold purchase plan is expected to operate. According to the theory, the rise in the commodity price level in this country must *parallel* the increase in the price of gold, or—what is the same thing—the depreciation of the paper dollar in the foreign exchanges. Some advocates of the theory admit, however, that there might be a slight lag in the adjustment of prices. They also point out that changes in the world value of gold would tend to accentuate or lessen the extent of the price rise caused by changes in the price of gold; but they contend that such changes can be offset by manipulation of the price of gold.

II. EFFICACY OF THE PLAN

This experiment in price regulation is strongly supported by a number of economists and business leaders. On the other hand, it is vigorously condemned by many economists and men of affairs. What light does actual experience shed on the possible efficacy of the plan and on the validity of the theory which underlies it?

At various times many countries have had depreciated exchanges and a consequent enhancement of the price of gold in terms of their national paper money units. In recent years, moreover, a number of countries have permanently devalued their currency units. Have commodity price levels in these countries shown a tendency to adjust themselves quickly and in precise proportion to changes in the price of gold? A few typical cases will be examined.

[5] George F. Warren and Frank A. Pearson, *Prices*, p. 164.

A. Experience of Six Countries

Great Britain and Sweden abandoned the gold standard in September 1931, and Japan in December of that year. The depreciation of their currency units, the accompanying changes in the price of gold, and the movements of wholesale commodity prices are shown in the following table, for the 18-month period prior to the depreciation of the American dollar.

PRICE EXPERIENCE OF THREE COUNTRIES UNDER
DEPRECIATED CURRENCY

Country	Currency Unit as a Percentage of Gold Parity (March 1933)	Price of Gold in Domestic Currency March 1933 (Par of Exchange = 100)	Wholesale Price Index, March 1933 (September 1931 = 100)
Great Britain.	70	143	99
Sweden......	68	147	98
Japan........	43	233	119

In Great Britain and Sweden, although the currency depreciated by roughly 30 per cent, which means a rise in the price of gold of more than 40 per cent, there was a slight decline in the level of comodity prices. In Japan the price of gold more than doubled; yet the general level of commodity prices registered a rise of only 19 per cent.

The failure of commodity price levels in Great Britain, Sweden, and Japan to respond fully to the rise in the price of gold, as measured by the depreciation of the pound, the krona, and the yen, cannot be explained by a corresponding rise in the *world value* of gold during the 18 months in question. Changes in the world value of gold would be indicated by the movement of commodity prices in countries still on the gold standard, the most important of which were the United States and France. During this period prices in the United States fell by 16 per cent, and in France by 18 per cent. With allowance for this factor the commodity price levels in Great Britain and Sweden should, in accordance with the theory, have been approximately 120 instead of 99 and 98 respectively, and in Japan about 190 instead of 119. With reference to Great Britain and Sweden the most that can be said is that depreciation of the currency and the consequent rise in the price of gold prevented as large a decline in commodity prices as might otherwise have occurred during that period. In the case of Japan, an enormous rise in the price of gold was accompanied merely by a very moderate rise in the commodity price level.

The recent experience of the United States shows results similar to those just indicated. The foreign exchange rate of the dollar ceased to be stable on April 20. The changes in the price of gold and in the general commodity price level during the seven months subsequent to that date are shown in the chart on page 118. Weekly averages are used for both sets of data. The maximum rise in the price of gold amounted to 65 per cent; the maximum rise in the commodity level was just under 20 per cent.

It remains to examine the experience of such countries as France and Italy, which have for some years been operating on the basis of *devalued* currency units. Since 1927 the gold content of the French franc has been fixed at almost exactly one-fifth of the pre-war weight. According to the theory the commodity price level should have become almost five times that of the United States (which was based on an unchanged currency unit) and should have moved during the six years 1927-32

in exact proportion with American prices at the ratio of
five to one. Similarly, the Italian lira has had a gold
content equal to slightly less than one-fourth of its pre-
war weight; hence the Italian price level should have

U. S. Wholesale Price Index Compared with Price of
Gold, April-November 1933

(Weekly averages. First week in April = 100)

adjusted itself at about four times the American level.

An assertion to the effect that this is precisely what
has occurred is found in the recent book by Warren and
Pearson referred to above.[6] However, the data which
they present on page 17 and show graphically on page
171 of their book do not support this assertion. While

[6] "France reduced the weight of gold in the franc so that her prices are
about five times pre-war when prices in the United States are at pre-war.
. . . Italy reduced the weight of gold in the lira so that her price level is
nearly 400 when prices in the United States are 100." The same, p. 171.

French and Italian prices have in fact been much higher than American prices the ratios have shown neither uniformity nor mathematical precision. As shown by the Warren and Pearson diagram, the ratio between the French and American price levels varied, during the years 1927-32, from 4.2:1 to 4.4:1; the ratio between the Italian and American price levels fluctuated between 3.0:1 and 3.6:1.

It is evident that whether the period of depreciation of the currency unit has been only a few months, as in the United States, or a year and a half as in Great Britain, Sweden, and Japan, there is no close correspondence between changes in the price of gold and changes in the comodity price level. Even over a period of years following a definitive devaluation of currency units, when any lagging tendency would be completely overcome, there is no mathematically precise relationship between commodity prices and the reduced content of the currency unit.

B. The Complex Character of Price Adjustments

The price *level* is merely a composite of the prices of individual commodities and groups of commodities. A change in the price of gold can, therefore, affect the price level only through changes which it might produce in the prices of individual commodities and groups of commodities. Hence, unless the effect of currency depreciation is to exert a uniform influence upon the prices of all classes of commodities or to raise some groups of prices sufficiently above the new level to offset the failure of other groups to rise proportionally, there is no reason to expect a mathematical adjustment of the movement of the price level to the depreciation of the currency unit.

The diverse character of price movements accompanying depreciation is illustrated by experience in Sweden. A detailed study of the effects of currency depreciation on commodity prices in that country recently led a competent Swedish investigator to conclude:

The depreciation of the Swedish krona after the abandonment of the gold standard has brought with it increases in price for certain imported goods; a check in the fall of prices for certain other international goods; but a merely retarded fall for a third group, mainly consisting of exports. In the case of purely domestic commodities, the falling tendency has made itself almost generally felt to about the same degree as before.[7]

It is not difficult to explain why currency depreciation should affect the prices of different groups of commodities in such varying degrees. As has already been shown, when gold is abandoned as the standard, or when the weight of the monetary unit is reduced, the change is manifested in foreign exchange quotations. Hence the depreciation of a currency in the foreign exchanges exerts a direct influence upon the prices of those commodities which enter into international trade. When a country's exchange rate declines, the prices of imports and exports tend to rise in terms of the national currency.

For example, Americans who import goods from abroad have to pay for their purchases in foreign currencies, and when the exchange value of the dollar depreciates they have to offer more paper dollars than before for the same amounts of foreign currencies. Hence, if they are not to suffer loss they must mark up

[7] Erik Lindahl, *The Consumption Price Index of the Bank of Sweden* (a mimeographed manuscript), Stockholm, April 1933. Between September 1931 and March 1933, the price index for imported commodities rose 15 per cent; that for exported commodities remained stationary; that for domestic industrial products declined 3 per cent; and that for domestic agricultural commodities fell by 17 per cent.

the selling price of the imported goods. It will be evident also that in so far as higher priced imported materials are used in domestic manufacture one element of cost is raised which tends to produce a rise in the price of the goods affected.

The effect of currency depreciation on the prices of goods exported from the country works out in a somewhat different manner. In general, when the dollar depreciates in the foreign exchanges, the foreign currencies will, immediately speaking, buy more American goods than before. The result is a stimulation of demand for American exports and a possible rise in their prices as expressed in paper dollars. The rise in the early stages is usually swift because speculators hasten to buy up exportable commodities in anticipation of the price rise. These effects appear with special rapidity in the case of such important staples as wheat, cotton, and tobacco, which are sold in well-organized international markets. The prices of such commodities are particularly subject to speculative influences, and daily price quotations concerning them are highly sensitive to many influences, including the rate of foreign exchange.

There are, however, certain factors which tend to limit the extent to which the prices of both import and export commodities will respond to changes in the foreign exchange rate. On the import side if sales to the United States are not to be curtailed by rising prices, foreigners in many cases may feel constrained to reduce their basic prices. In the case of exports the demand for American products is stimulated only so long as the price rise is less than the amount of exchange depreciation; when prices rise to the full extent of the depreciation there is no longer any competitive advantage in buying here rather than elsewhere. Even before this occurs, the advantage obtained by American exporters might tend to be counteracted by special trade barriers put up by the importing countries, by enforced price cutting on the part of competing countries, or by parallel depreciation of foreign currencies. It is limiting factors such as these which explain the failure of both import and export prices in a country with depreciated currency to rise in any precise relationship to the depreciation, and to exert any predictable upward influence on the general price level.

The depreciation of the exchange rate has only an indirect influence upon the prices of those commodities which are produced and consumed domestically. For example, in the production of automobiles the largest elements of cost are labor and domestically produced materials. Wages are not immediately affected by exchange depreciation and the cost of domestically produced materials is directly affected only in case such materials are also produced for export, as in the case of cotton. The costs of automobile manufacture would thus in no way be proportionally increased; and hence it would not be necessary for the price to be advanced proportionally to the currency depreciation in order to maintain profits. Nor would the purchasing power with which to buy higher priced automobiles be immediately available.

It is only gradually that the prices of goods, produced domestically and consumed mainly within the country, feel any effect from exchange depreciation. The rising prices of goods entering into international trade come, in some measure and with the passage of time, to affect domestic prices generally, through increasing costs; and

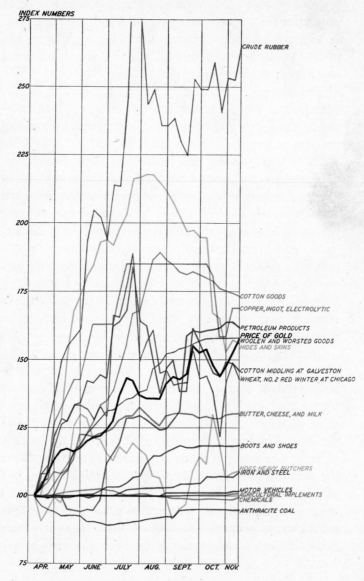

INDEX NUMBERS
275

250

225

200

175

150

125

100

75

APR.   MAY   JUNE   JULY   AUG.   SEPT.   OCT.   NOV.

CRUDE RUBBER

COTTON GOODS

COPPER, INGOT, ELECTROLYTIC

PETROLEUM PRODUCTS
PRICE OF GOLD
WOOLEN AND WORSTED GOODS
HIDES AND SKINS

COTTON MIDDLING AT GALVESTON
WHEAT, NO. 2 RED WINTER AT CHICAGO

BUTTER, CHEESE, AND MILK

BOOTS AND SHOES

HOGS, HEAVY, BUTCHERS
IRON AND STEEL

MOTOR VEHICLES
AGRICULTURAL IMPLEMENTS
CHEMICALS

ANTHRACITE COAL

in due course wage rates also have to be adjusted upward. The possible influence of changes in the price of gold upon the prices of commodities which are not directly affected by exchange depreciation is thus even less precise and less predictable than in the case of exported and imported commodities.

The diversity in the movements of prices of 16 important individual commodities and groups of commodities in the United States since the dollar began to depreciate is graphically indicated by the accompanying chart. It will be noted that the prices of coal and chemicals have declined since April, and that the prices of iron and steel, automobiles, and agricultural implements have risen but little. The prices of other commodities have shown a wide range of fluctuation, some of them remaining persistently below the price of gold, some maintaining a position above it, and some swinging up and down without any apparent relation to it. The largest fluctuations have occurred in the prices of such highly sensitive and speculative international commodities as rubber, wheat, cotton, and hides.

The effects of speculation may be inferred from this chart, as well as from the chart on page 118, where the movement of the price of gold is shown in relation to the general wholesale price index. Speculative influences were extremely active during the first three months of the period under examination, that is, until the middle of July. The prices of many important commodities were the period under examination, that is, until the middle of July. The prices of many important commodities were then rising rapidly, and the general price level was moving upward. Since the middle of July, there has been little, if any, correspondence between the two movements. Apparently speculation had spent most of its force.

The chart opposite page 123 illustrates the complexity of the commodity price structure. The price-making process is also extremely complex in character, and the movements of the price level are subject to a large variety of influences other than the price of gold. Even if one were to grant that the simple gold theory of commodity prices might possibly be valid in a community using gold as its only form of money, that theory is wholly inapplicable to the complex modern world, in which the monetary supply consists primarily of credit instruments and in which the course of commodity prices is greatly affected by the state of business psychology, the interaction between credit and fiscal policies and general economic conditions, and many other monetary and non-monetary factors.

In this connection, it should be borne in mind that in the United States numerous other devices for stimulating a rise in prices are being currently utilized. For example, the output of certain agricultural commodities is being curtailed by the Agricultural Adjustment Administration; costs of manufacture are being raised by the National Recovery Administration; and purchasing power is being expanded through the expenditure of public funds in connection with public works and relief activities. At the same time the policy of cheapening credit through open market operations and other devices has also been followed.

Even if one were to argue that these policies, singly or conjointly, have had no effect whatever in raising prices in the United States, and that the rise which has occurred is the result solely of the depreciation of the dollar, it still remains true that the extent of the rise in

the general level of prices shows little correspondence
with the rise in the price of gold. The great disparity between the two movements furnishes conclusive evidence
that the theory of automatic adjustments between
changes in the price of gold and changes in the commodity price level is without scientific validity. As a
practical matter, the most that can be said for the theory
is that the depreciation of the currency may, under conditions at present existing in the United States, help to
bring the prices of some agricultural commodities entering into export trade, which have been heavily depressed, into a more satisfactory adjustment with other
prices. As we shall see in the next chapter, however, a
monetary policy based on the depreciation of the currency
unit has far-reaching economic repercussions.

The foregoing analysis leads to two primary conclusions: The first is that no definite, predictable rise in
the commodity price level can be assumed to follow a
given depreciation of the currency. Such rise as occurs
is not general or horizontal in character, representing
an automatic adjustment of all commodity prices to alterations in the price of gold. The price changes that take
place begin with commodities passing into international
commerce, and even these changes do not necessarily
correspond closely with the depreciation of the currency.
Their effect upon the general level of costs and prices
within the country is indirect and, at best, slow. The
extent to which the general domestic price level will rise
is affected by a large variety of factors in the general
business and fiscal situation, and the specific influence of
currency depreciation cannot be dissociated from the operation of these other factors.

The second conclusion is that, once a desired price

level had been obtained, by whatever means, no evidence exists that thenceforth that level can be automatically controlled by altering the price of gold. This is because the theory assumes that the commodity price level changes in direct proportion to changes in the price of gold, such changes representing an automatic revaluation of commodities. Our analysis of the experience of a number of countries clearly indicates that no such automatic revaluation occurs. Whether other machinery for controlling the level of prices offers a better chance of success is beyond the scope of this inquiry.[8]

[8] A more detailed analysis of the relation of currency depreciation and devaluation to commodity prices and to foreign trade will be given in forthcoming Brookings Institution studies on these subjects.

CHAPTER VII

THE TWO MAJOR ISSUES

As at Geneva in January, at Washington in April and May, and at London in June and July, two major issues continue to dominate monetary discussion today. The first is whether economic recovery can be effectively promoted by raising commodity prices through monetary action. The second is whether the restoration of an international monetary organization is essential to world prosperity. What light does the present American policy throw on the first issue, and what is its relation to the second issue?

The first issue is now being tested, on a national scale, in the United States, and the depreciation of the dollar in the foreign exchanges is being employed as the principal instrument of monetary action for the purpose of raising commodity prices. As has just been indicated, a price rise of some degree has accompanied the carrying out of this policy. On the assumption that the rise has been the result solely, or at least in large measure, of currency depreciation, it might be argued that the policy has been in some measure already justified. This is, however, only one side of the story.

The evidence presented in the preceding chapter shows conclusively that there is no assured and predictable relationship between the depreciation of the currency unit and the commodity price level. If the theory underlying the gold purchase plan were valid, and a 20 per cent depreciation of the dollar could be definitely counted on to raise the commodity price level by 20 per cent within a predictable period of time, we would know precisely to what extent it would be necessary to increase the price of gold in order to give us the price level desired. But since the extent of the commodity price rise is altogether unpredictable, no one can possibly know how far the price of gold might have to be raised to achieve the desired result, nor how long a period of time might be involved in the process. The inescapable result is monetary uncertainty.

I. IMPLICATIONS OF MONETARY UNCERTAINTY

The effects of monetary uncertainty upon economic life have been clearly revealed in post-war experience. The economic repercussions manifest themselves principally in connection with international trade, the capital market, and government credit.

The depreciation of currency units in the foreign exchanges affects international trade in a number of ways. The uncertainty with respect to the value of currencies increases the risk in the short-term credit operations upon upon which the conduct of foreign trade so largely depends, and leads to an almost complete cessation of long-term investment. The consequence is a curtailment of trade.

The artificial stimulus to exports resulting from a depreciated currency leads sooner or later to retaliatory action on the part of other countries—retaliation which may take the form of higher tariffs, import licenses, quota systems, or competition in the business of currency depreciation. The experience of the last two years is replete with examples of such action. The cumulative effect has been to demoralize international trade in general and with it the production of wealth everywhere. Instead of making it possible for men and women in all countries to produce commodities and trade with the people of other countries, these policies have served to increase unemployment and impoverishment.

The effects of monetary uncertainty are of equal importance in connection with the so-called capital market. It is recognized that a full employment of labor and thorough business recovery cannot be expected until the construction of capital goods is resumed. The resumption of capital enterprise depends in large measure upon the resumption of normal issues of long-term securities. In the presence of an uncertain monetary policy the flotation of such securities is unquestionably deterred. While this problem is complicated by other factors, monetary instability is clearly an important contributing cause.

Finally, experience shows that monetary uncertainty sooner or later leads to a deterioration of government credit. So long as the uncertainty prevails, potential investors hesitate to purchase fixed income securities of all kinds, including those issued by the government. Outstanding government issues decline in value, with resulting repercussions upon the banking structure and the investment markets.

In the United States at the present time the maintenance of government credit is of especial importance because of its relation to other phases of the general recovery plan. Public loans must be floated if the necessary funds are to be available for carrying out the program of public works, as well as the numerous relief, housing, and agricultural projects now under way. Difficulty in borrowing might force the government either to curtail these projects or to embark upon the issuance of greenback currency as an alternative means of meeting its financial obligations and requirements.

Past experience in many countries has invariably shown that when a government resorts to the printing press for fiscal purposes, monetary uncertainty becomes greatly intensified, the flight of capital from the country is accelerated, and the depreciation of the currency in the foreign exchange becomes increasingly difficult to control. It should be borne in mind in this connection that, largely because of its psychological effects, the issuance of greenbacks would have an influence upon the foreign exchange value of the dollar similar to that of an increase in the price paid for gold.

It is outside the scope of this survey to discuss the possibilities of raising prices through monetary action on an international, rather than national, scale. The London session of the World Monetary and Economic Conference showed conclusively that a concerted international policy of price-raising by means of monetary action is today out of the question. Hence the price-raising program now being carried out by the government in this country appears likely to remain national in scope. This character of the American monetary policy has vital economic implications, alike for this country and for the rest of the world.

II. THE FUTURE OF MONETARY ORGANIZATION

With reference to the second issue, it is clear that the following out of the present American policy would mean disruption of international monetary organization. The effort to raise American prices by independent monetary action makes it impossible for the world as a whole to establish stable exchanges and to restore the normal functioning of an international monetary system. Moreover, if after prices reach the desired level, an effort should be made to maintain stability of that level by manipulating the weight of the dollar, stable foreign exchanges would be automatically debarred.

It will be recalled from the analysis in Chapter I that the only practical means of maintaining stable foreign exchanges is through the operation of an international gold standard based upon fixed gold ratios, unlimited redemption of paper currency in gold at a fixed rate for purposes of international payments, an unlimited market for gold at a fixed price, and free exports and imports of the metal. The first three of these conditions obviously cannot be fulfilled under the compensated dollar plan.

From the discussion presented in Chapter II, it is clear that the issue between an international monetary system and nationally managed currencies is one of profound economic significance. The emphasis in the first is on the stability of national currency units in terms of gold, and, therefore, of foreign exchanges; in the second, on stability of national price levels, with fluctuating currency units and unstable foreign exchanges. Under an international monetary system, economic equilibrium and relative stability of commodity prices would be sought primarily in an adjustment of underlying economic factors and processes, rather than through monetary manipulation; under dissociated national systems, monetary action, directed toward a stabilization of price levels, would be relied upon as a primary means of regulating economic activity. The first is designed to serve as a foundation for a system of international economic intercourse; the second, under existing political conditions, presupposes, as its inevitable corollary, an organization of the world based on economic nationalism.

International monetary organization based on stable foreign exchanges will be impossible if the United States should finally decide against adherence to the gold standard in the future. It would be similarly impossible if Great Britain were to make such a decision. At the end of the World War, the determination of these two greatest commercial and financial nations of the world to restore the gold standard settled the issue. The temporary recalcitrance of France and of the other nations which delayed their return to gold could have a complicating, but not a decisive, influence.

In this second post-war period of monetary unsettlement in which the world finds itself today, the international center of gravity in monetary policy was in Great Britain from the time that country abandoned the gold standard in September 1931, to the spring of 1933. Since then, it has definitely shifted to the United States. Upon this country's final decision in the sphere of monetary policy will largely depend the character of the world's monetary and economic organization in the future.

The continued monetary uncertainty and economic instability at the end of 1933 suggest the need of a reconsideration of monetary policies in relation to economic recovery, both nationally and internationally. The point of departure for such a reconsideration might well be a renewed study of the analyses and recommendations of the Geneva Commission of Experts, drawn up at the beginning of the year.

DOCUMENTARY APPENDIXES

APPENDIX A

MONETARY DISCUSSION IN THE ANNOTATED AGENDA[1]

I. MONETARY AND CREDIT POLICY

The Lausanne Conference laid special emphasis on the necessity of restoring currencies to a healthy basis and, in this connection, the restoration of a satisfactory international monetary standard is clearly of primary importance. The World Conference, in the absence of another international standard likely to be universally acceptable, will have to consider how the conditions for a successful restoration of a free gold standard could be fulfilled. In our view, among the essential conditions, which are discussed more fully below, are the restoration of equilibrium between prices and costs and, in the future, such a reasonable degree of stability of prices as the world measure of value should properly possess.

The time when it will be possible for a particular country to return to the gold standard and the exchange parity at which such a return can safely be made will necessarily depend on the conditions in that country as well as those abroad, and these questions can only be determined by the proper authorities in each country separately.

In the following sections, we set forth a series of suggestions of a general nature which would seem calculated to facilitate the work of the conference on the monetary side. It will be found that some of these suggestions can only be put into effect through concerted action, while others call for the individual effort of particular countries.

1. Conditions under Which a Restoration of a Free International Gold Standard Would be Possible

a) We would lay stress upon what has already been indicated in the introduction—that the solution of major outstanding po-

[1] League of Nations Document No. C. 48. M. 18. 1933. II. [Conf. M.E.I.].

litical problems would contribute to that restoration of confidence without which great hesitation will be felt in taking decisions to return to the gold standard.

b) In the second place, a series of measures would have to be taken in order to make it possible for countries whose reserves are at present inadequate to attain a satisfactory reserve position:

i) A settlement of inter-governmental debts would be of particular value in this respect;

ii) A return to a reasonable degree of freedom in the movement of goods and services;

iii) A return to freedom in the foreign exchange markets and in the movement of capital.

c) There should be a general understanding about measures to ensure a better working of the gold standard in the future. Success in obtaining an understanding of this character will not only be a factor of potent influence on public opinion in many countries, but will also give the assurance to an individual country that, as long as it pursues a sound monetary and economic policy, it will be in a position to acquire and maintain the necessary reserves.

d) International action, however indispensable, cannot restore a normal economic situation unless the proper internal measures have been taken. Each individual country must therefore be prepared to take the necessary steps to achieve internal equilibrium in the following matters:

i) Revenue and expenditure, not only of the state budget proper, but also of the budgets of public enterprises (railways, etc.) and of local authorities, should be balanced;

ii) It will be necessary to create and maintain healthy conditions in the internal money and capital market and at all costs to avoid an inflationary increase of the note circulation in order to meet government deficits;

iii) It is necessary to give that sufficient degree of flexibility to the national economy without which an international monetary standard, however improved, cannot function properly.

We feel that, in practice, certain countries are in a key position in that the re-establishment of a free gold standard by them would influence action in a number of other countries.

We are well aware of the difficulty, for countries no longer on the gold standard, of returning to that standard at an appropriate rate of exchange, so long as uncertainty prevails with regard to the course of gold prices. The experience of the last decade has shown that the restoration of the gold standard at too low a rate of exchange as well as at too high a rate presents grave disadvantages, not only from the national, but also from the international, point of view. On the other hand, the very fact that exchanges continue to fluctuate is not without its effect on the level of gold prices and may hamper a monetary and economic policy designed to promote a recovery of prices in gold countries. In the face of this dilemma it would appear necessary to consider what policy may best be pursued in the immediate future in order to bring about such a general recovery as would facilitate the re-establishment of the international monetary standard.

2. Currency Policy to be followed prior to such a General Restoration of the Gold Standard

It will be useful to consider what specific measures must be taken in different groups of countries.

a) *Countries with a free gold standard and with abundant monetary reserves:*

i) To pursue a liberal credit policy, characterised by low money rates in the short-term market and a reduction of long-term money rates by conversions and other operations as far as feasible;

ii) As far as market conditions and central bank statutes permit, to maintain an open market policy designed to provide a plentiful supply of credit;

iii) To allow gold to flow out freely;

iv) To permit the greatest freedom possible to outward capital movements in order to facilitate sound foreign investments.

b) *Countries which have left the gold standard:*

i) Efforts should be made to avoid a competition between states to acquire a temporary advantage in international trade by depreciating the external value of their currency below such a point as is required to re-establish internal equilibrium;

ii) Under present conditions, exchange rates are liable to be constantly disturbed by speculative movements to the disadvantage of international trade. In a period prior to the adoption of a new parity, it is advisable for the authorities regulating the currencies concerned to smooth out, so far as their resources permit, day-to-day fluctuations in the exchanges due to speculative influences by buying and selling foreign currencies. The success of such measures would be enhanced by the co-operation of other markets.

c) *Countries which have introduced exchange restrictions, whether they have abandoned the gold standard or not:*

i) It is desirable that these restrictions should be totally abolished as early as possible. It is realised, however, that this ultimate aim cannot in all cases be immediately attained. In such circumstances, the restrictions applied to foreign trade should be relaxed or abolished in the first instance, even though it may be necessary to maintain them for a time with regard to capital movements. (This whole question is referred to more fully in Section III, 1.)

ii) Such relaxation may, in certain cases where the external value of the currency has depreciated, necessitate the abandonment of existing parities. In a number of countries, exchange restrictions would seem to defeat their own end; for, whenever the official rate of exchange is maintained at a higher level than the economic rate, a form of import premium is given to all importers and a form of export duty imposed on all exporters. Experience seems to have proved that, when a careful policy of gradually relaxing restrictions is pursued, internal confidence in the currency can be maintained, although, of course, in such circumstances, the necessity of effecting budgetary equilibrium and of resisting inflationary tendencies will prove to be of paramount importance. In such cases, it would seem particularly valuable to maintain a close relationship between these countries, the Financial Organisation of the League and the Bank for International Settlements, in order to devise and apply the appropriate policy in each case.

In the case of certain countries which are heavily indebted abroad, more especially on short-term, a solution of the debt problem is necessary before their governments will be in a position to modify existing monetary policy. We deal with this question later.

3. Functioning of the Gold Standard

It is important that any declarations in favour of the restoration of an international gold standard should, at the same time, indicate certain essential principles for its proper functioning under modern conditions.

It is not our intention to suggest that anything should be done which would in any way limit the freedom of action and reduce the responsibility of central banks in determining monetary policy. The following statement is in full agreement with the report of the Gold Delegation, which we endorse. This report has also been endorsed by the Board of the Bank for International Settlements. The governments will no doubt find opportunity to consult their central banks on these questions before taking their final decision at the conference.

a) *Relation between political authorities and central banks:* We would suggest that the conference emphasise the importance of the monetary organisation being so arranged as to make central banks independent of political influence. We feel it also important to suggest that governments in their economic and financial policy should avoid increasing the difficulties of central banks in the discharge of their responsibility.

b) *Monetary reserves:* The modern tendency is to concentrate gold in central banks. Before the war, more than 40 per cent of the total monetary gold stocks consisted of gold in circulation or with private banks, while, at the present time, only 9 per cent represents gold not in the hands of central banks. This development is, in our opinion, to be welcomed, as it tends to enhance the power and the freedom of action of central banks. Gold reserves are now primarily required to meet external demands for payment caused by some disequilibrium on the foreign account. At the same time it must be recognized that present-day legislation in many countries renders much gold unavailable for international use. We believe that the following steps can be taken—without in any way diminishing public confidence—in order to permit more effective use of the reserves of central banks:

i) *Lowering of cover ratios.*—Experience during the past few years has clearly shown that the cover provisions in the statutes of many central banks have not been sufficiently elastic to permit the utilisation of reserves for meeting foreign payments to an extent which would be justified in cases of emergency.

The increased volume of short-term funds capable of moving rapidly from one country to another may represent an extra burden on the balance of payments.

Moreover, when the national economy has, for one reason or another, become less flexible, it may take longer to restore a lost equilibrium and during the intervening period a larger amount of gold may have to be exported.

We suggest that the conference should stress the need of introducing greater elasticity in the primary cover regulations of central banks, particularly so as to make the reserves more fully available to meet fluctuations in the balance of payments.

A great advance would be made if legal minimum requirements of gold (or of gold and foreign exchange) were substantially lowered below the customary 33 or 40 ratio. The margin available for payments abroad—representing the difference between the actual holdings and the legal minimum—would then be considerably greater. However, the conference should—it is suggested—emphasise strongly that a change in the minimum cover requirements must not be taken by countries with limited resources as an excuse for the building up of a larger superstructure of notes and credits, for then the free margin would be dissipated and the purpose of the reform—the strengthening of the position of the central bank concerned—would not be achieved.

ii) *The gold exchange standard.*—In addition to those countries which allow foreign exchange to be included in their legal reserve requirements, central banks in nearly all countries supplement their gold holdings with foreign short-term assets in order to be able to influence the exchange more directly and more speedily than by gold exports. In some cases, central banks also employ those assets to influence their internal money markets.

This system as practised in recent years, particularly when it has involved the maintenance of very considerable exchange holdings, has not worked without revealing some grave defects. The exceptional circumstances of these years undoubtedly contributed to an undue accumulation of foreign balances in particular markets. We think that these defects may be overcome partly by the better working of the gold standard itself and partly by special improvements which would provide for a system more centralised and subject to more effective control. We are of the opinion that this system of holding foreign exchange balances, if properly controlled, may for many countries hasten their return to an international standard and will form an essential feature in the permanent financial arrangements of the countries which have no highly developed capital markets. It is very desirable that foreign exchange holdings in central banks should be invested with or through the central bank of the currency concerned or with the Bank for International Settlements. This is all the more important, because it is, in our opinion, imperative that central banks should have a complete knowledge of all the operations of other central banks on their markets. Moreover, it is important that each central bank which employs foreign exchange balances should take all necessary measures in order to secure itself against the risks of foreign investments.

iii) *Other methods of economising gold.*—In countries where bank notes of small denominations are in circulation, these small notes may be withdrawn and replaced within proper limits by subsidiary coin, which will to some extent reduce the strain on gold reserves through the decrease in note circulation.

It should further be possible to improve the mechanism of clearing in individual countries. Payments of taxes and salaries, large retail transactions, the transference of money from place to place, may increasingly be effected by means of cheques, post-office payments or other transfers, and much could be done by governments and municipal authorities, even without legislation, to set an example by accepting cheques in payments for taxes, public utility services, etc.

iv) *Distribution of monetary reserves.*—The present abnormal gold situation, with nearly 80 per cent of the world's monetary gold concentrated in five countries, cannot be explained by any single factor, but should be regarded as a sign of certain profound disequilibria which have influenced the numerous elements in the balance of payments. When considering remedies, the multiplicity of the causes must be taken into account. To obtain a more lasting improvement of present abnormal conditions it will be necessary to allow a freer movement of goods and to rely less upon gold shipments for the settlement of foreign liabilities.

In previous sections of this document, we have suggested that the minimum cover requirements of central banks should be lowered and have also expressed the opinion that some countries should allow holdings of foreign exchange to be included in the legal reserves. The difficulties connected with the uneven distribution of gold in the world will to some extent be mitigated by these measures; but they are, of course, not in themselves sufficient.

When countries with deficient reserves return to the gold standard, the new parities should be such as to be consistent with a favourable balance of payments and so attract an adequate reserve without undue effort.

In some cases, an automatic adjustment of the situation will take place by a return movement of previously expatriated capital, which has been invested in countries with large monetary reserves. It is important that public opinion in the latter countries should realise that an outflow of gold under such circumstances does not in itself reveal a disequilibrium in the balance of payments, but is rather a sign of a general revival of confidence. To prevent an outflow by credit restriction might not only retard the redistribution of gold, but might also have a deflationary tendency.

The question arises whether it would not be possible to anticipate, by international credit operations, the process of building up adequate reserves in countries where these reserves are now deficient. Such operations might relieve the foreign exchange markets of the prolonged strain which would be inflicted on them by a continuous demand for gold by central banks desirous of strengthening their reserves (see below under III, 3).

c) *Co-operation of central banks in credit policy:* The conference will no doubt wish to emphasise the great importance to be attached to the maintenance of close relationship between central banks which will permit them to take account of both national and international considerations when framing their policy. While the responsibility of each one of them for the measures taken on their own markets must be left unimpaired, continuous consultations between them should help to co-ordinate the policy pursued in the various centres and may indeed enable the intervention of an individual bank to become more effective if supported from abroad.

The Bank for International Settlements represents a new agency for central banks and should be able to play an increasingly important part, not only by improving contact, but also as an instrument for common action, of which several indications can be found in this document.

In this connection, we draw the attention to point 5 of the resolution which the Board of the Bank for International Settlements, at its meeting on July 11th, 1932, unanimously adopted. The board declared itself in substantial agreement with the conclusions of the final report of the Gold Delegation of the League of Nations of June 1932. These conclusions were considered by the board as forming a starting-point for the elaboration of monetary principles which may be given practical application in future.

We attach great importance to this declaration and to the pursuance of consultations among central banks, particularly with a view to achieving the object, as stated in the report of the Gold Delegation, of checking undue fluctuations in the purchasing power of gold. We are convinced, as were the Gold Delegation, that action must be based on international understanding and co-operation. The prospects of the general restoration of the gold standard and of its successful working in the future appear to depend in large measure on progress in this field.

4. Silver

After keeping relatively stable from 1921 to 1929, the price of silver in gold currencies fell abruptly by more than one-half in less than three years. There is no doubt that this sudden decline must, in the main, be attributed to the same causes as have acted on the general level of prices and may thus be said to illustrate in a particular case the incidence of the world depression. Some special factors can, however, be found which have accentuated the downward trend, and these were to some extent already operating before the depression set in. Such factors are:

the demonetisation of silver, the reduction of the silver content of token coins, and also the disposal of surplus stocks.

We have considered a series of proposals which have been discussed in recent years with a view to raising the price of silver, and we wish, in this connection, to make the following observations:

i) It has been suggested that some form of bimetallism should be introduced.

We would point out that a bimetallic standard, which presupposes a fixed relation between the value of gold and that of silver, could be safely introduced only if the most important countries of the world agreed to such a measure. As the only international monetary standard which is at present likely to command universal acceptance is the gold standard, the idea of introducing bimetallism must be regarded as impracticable.

ii) It has been proposed that banks of issue should be allowed to hold increased quantities of silver in their legal reserves.

On the assumption that no form of bimetallism will prove acceptable, silver is unsuitable for extensive inclusion in the metallic reserves of a central bank, there being no fixed price at which it would be received by other central banks in the settlement of balances on the international account.

iii) It has also been suggested that governmental action should be taken for the purpose of improving the price of silver.

We would, in this connection, refer to the suggestion made in a previous part of this report to the effect that, in countries where bank notes of small denominations are in circulation, these small notes might be withdrawn and replaced within proper limits by subsidiary coins, and we think that the conference should, in this connection, examine to what extent the use of silver in subsidiary coinage could be enlarged. Whatever sales of government stocks of silver may be deemed desirable, it is important to conduct these in such a manner as to avoid any unnecessary disturbance of the market.

The conference should also consider whether, and if so by what methods, the marketing of the metal by producers and currency authorities is susceptible of improvement. The question of developing new and enlarged industrial uses for silver is in our judgment also worthy of careful consideration.

From the point of view of commercial relations with silver-using countries, particularly China, trade interests would best be served, not by a rise in the price of silver as such, but by a rise in the general level of commodity prices. Any action which would tend to raise that level and in due course achieve its stabilisation may be expected to have a favourable effect on the price of silver and would, on general grounds, be welcome.

II. PRICES

1. Disequilibrium between Prices and Costs

The decline in prices of recent years has created a series of difficulties which must, by one method or another, be overcome in order to make progress in the monetary and economic field possible.

In the first place, the burden of debts has increased considerably in terms of real wealth and made it more and more difficult for debtors to discharge their obligations and avoid a breach of contract. With regard to internal debts, a special transfer problem arises, with possible dangerous repercussions on the whole monetary structure.

Secondly, as a rule, costs fall more slowly than prices, which tends to make enterprises unremunerative, with a consequent disorganisation and reduction of production as evidenced by an increase of unemployment. Even if unemployment benefits are granted, the reduction in earnings will, in its turn, diminish the purchasing power in the hands of the public. Moreover, a restriction of sales will make further sound extension—or even the upkeep—of industrial plant seem unnecessary and arrest activity with regard to new investments, causing, not only particularly serious unemployment for workers engaged in producing capital goods, but also a tendency for savings to remain idle.

Thirdly, the decline in prices has not proceeded at the same pace for all classes of commodities. Manufactured articles tend, for many reasons, to fall more slowly in price than natural products, and it is a well-known fact that retail prices are more resistant than wholesale. A special feature of the present depression is the tendency revealed in a number of countries for prices of certain classes of goods required for capital equipment to resist a fall, such as would have facilitated readjustments. This tendency has retarded recovery and has rendered new capital enterprise unattractive, however low short- and long-term rates of interest may be. In some cases, the cause of this relative rigidity in the prices of investment goods would seem to be that they have, on the whole, been more controlled by cartels and other monopolistic combines than other goods.

The decline in production, superimposed on the decline in prices, has reduced the national money incomes of some of the largest countries in the world to less than 60 per cent of what they were three years ago. In countries which depend for their export on primary products, the gold prices of these products have in many cases fallen to a third, a quarter, or even less, of the former price. Depreciation of their currencies may to some extent have alleviated their internal difficulties, but the precipitous decline in world prices has had its disastrous effects on the foreign position of these countries, particularly by so substantially increasing the burden of their external liabilities.

Furthermore, difficult budgetary problems of great concern to governments have arisen—in particular, as grants for unemployment benefit and other social purposes are added to the expenditure. When the revenue of states and local authorities must be raised from a shrinking national income, rates of taxation will, after a certain point, become so high that they cannot but exert a serious depressing influence on trade and industry.

2. Methods of restoring Equilibrium

a) Obviously, one method of restoring a lost equilibrium between costs and prices is to reduce costs. As a rule, this will not be possible without reducing money rates of wages. Some considerable reductions of this kind have recently been effected, in certain countries to the extent of something like 20 to 25 per cent. It is found, however, that possibilities for effecting such reductions differ from one country to another, and that each further substantial reduction meets with increased resistance.

It is an open question, difficult to answer *a priori*, to what extent these reductions will correct former maladjustments between different categories of wages and prices (particularly in different stages of the process of production) and in that way bring about a better relative position. The burden of debts will, however, if left undiminished, create many difficult problems.

b) Equilibrium may also be restored by a rise in prices.

i) One method of raising prices is to limit supply. Reference is made to this subject in Section VI of these Annotations.

ii) In countries with a free gold standard and with large monetary reserves, it would seem possible (as indicated in Section I, 2a) to pursue a liberal credit policy, including low short-term interest rates and in some cases also open market operations. Moreover, there should be, as far as feasible, a reduction of long-term interest rates by means of conversions and other operations. It is pertinent to observe that the open market operations which were undertaken by the Federal Reserve Banks of the United States of America in the spring of 1932, in conjunction with the measures taken through the Reconstruction Finance Corporation, arrested the contraction of credits and the hoarding of currency; they also created excess reserves for private banks to an amount of more than $500 million, which helped to restore confidence in the banking structure.

Some central banks, by means of the leadership they exercise on their markets, have been able to induce savings banks and similar institutions to adjust deposit rates and at the same time bring down rates for mortgage loans and other long-term obligations.

iii) In order that a liberal credit policy may have the desired effect on prices, it is necessary that a demand for credit should arise.

In the first place, there is some reason to expect a spontaneous demand for goods. For example, during the depression, many industrial firms not only abstained from enlarging their plant but also postponed repairs. But this delay cannot go on indefinitely, and it is probable that, in this field, a considerable potential demand has accumulated. Many firms have in past years made financial provisions for this purpose on their depreciation account. Even consumers may be in a somewhat similar position as regards more durable articles, such as clothes, furniture, motor cars, etc.

The suggestion is often made that governments and other authorities should actively increase the purchasing power in the hands of the public by extensive schemes for public expenditure, financed by borrowings from the market. If such a policy were not kept within reasonable limits, and if it were to result in deteriorating government credit, debt conversions might be interfered with and the lowering of long-term interest rates delayed.

It is very much as an outcome of increasing confidence in the general financial and economic structure that we expect an increase in effective demand. If it is found that political and monetary authorities are endeavouring to carry out a policy which holds out some hope of ultimate improvement, we believe that the public will soon respond by resuming normal economic developments. We venture to suggest that a general adoption of the policy outlined in this report—aiming at the restoration of currencies on a healthy basis, financial reconstruction, a greater freedom in the movement of goods and some immediate measures to give evidence of its practical application—would be a decisive step towards this revival of confidence.

iv) Finally, a few words suffice to point out that a recovery of sound international lending, which would put purchasing power into the hands of countries with a limited supply of domestic capital, would have a helpful effect on prices.

III. RESUMPTION OF THE MOVEMENT OF CAPITAL

A return to a normal situation will be dependent, *inter alia*, on a resumption of international capital movements. It is essential that the obstacles which at the present moment prevent such a resumption be cleared away so that, when confidence returns, capital can move freely. Apart from the instability of exchanges, which we have dealt with above, some of the major obstacles to capital movements are the control of foreign exchanges and, in certain cases, the existing burden of debts.

1. Abolition of Foreign Exchange Restrictions

The adverse balance of accounts in many countries, aggravated by the drop in prices and the falling-off in foreign trade, has obliged those countries, when they could no longer re-establish equilibrium by means of foreign credits, to choose between abandoning the stability of their currency or instituting exchange restrictions as an artificial means of balancing imports and exports of foreign currency. Certain countries have even adopted both systems simultaneously. The majority of the countries which have recently suffered the disastrous consequences of unrestricted inflation have opted for exchange restrictions and have thus maintained the nominal parity of their currency. Such control has enabled them more or less successfully to prevent or limit exports of national capital and the withdrawal of foreign credits, but this result has been obtained only by closing the door to new investments. Further, foreign exchange restrictions have frequently been adopted in order to improve the balance of payments by refusing to pay in foreign currency for those imports which do not appear indispensable. But, in the long run, this reduction has not had the expected effect of improving the trade balance, since the exports from each country encounter similar monetary restrictions abroad or administrative barriers hastily erected as a measure of defence.

Thus, exchange restrictions, and clearing agreements which often follow, constitute an almost insurmountable obstacle to the circulation of capital, and represent one of the main causes of the falling-off in international trade. A return to normal conditions presupposes their disappearance, which is itself conditional, in each of the countries concerned, on the permanent restoration of equilibrium in the balance of payments.

In order to provide for the restoration of equilibrium in the balance of payments and to ensure permanence by strengthening the metal reserve of certain banks of issue, various measures are essential which have been mentioned above. It may be useful to stress the fact that it is not necessary in all cases to wait for the governments to meet before taking these measures. On the contrary, it is essential that, in every country, efforts should be made without delay with a view to the restoration of a normal situation.

2. Existing Indebtedness

It may happen that, when all the above mentioned measures have been taken, permanent equilibrium in the balance of payments cannot be restored owing to the threat of mass withdrawals of short-term deposits or owing to the heavy charge resulting from the service of long-term debts. In that event, arrangements relating to foreign debts will have to be made between the parties concerned.

We desire at this point to stress the fact that it is essential that the policy followed by the creditor countries should finally place the debtor countries in a position to pay off their obligations in the form of goods and services.

We also venture to state that the restoration of a normal situation must be accompanied by a return of confidence, and that, in this connection, respect for undertakings entered into is an essential factor. Only when, as a result of unforeseen circumstances, it has become impossible for contracts to be carried out in their entirety can an adjustment of obligations to the possibilities of the situation be effected between the parties concerned in the interests of creditors and debtors alike.

i) *Short-term debts:* The present regulation of the short-term debts of various countries by means of standstill agreements, exchange restrictions and transfer moratoria is in its very nature only a temporary measure. If applied for any length of time, such measures tend to prolong the crisis and to increase its intensity by delaying the moment when the situation will appear in its true light. That is why the existing system, which presents the danger of placing good and bad debtors on a footing of equality and thus tends to destroy the credit of the good debtors, should be brought to an end as soon as possible and be replaced by a definitive solution which would take into account the circumstances of each individual case. It is essential that this readjustment should have the effect of liberating real commercial acceptances as soon as possible from any form of regulation. Trade could thus revive by utilising its normal channels. The banks of issue in every country should support such a measure of restoration by every means in their power.

The settlement of this question is essentially the concern of the creditors and the debtors themselves. It is nevertheless important for governments that a solution should be found for this problem, which undoubtedly affects both the monetary and the commercial policy of the country. The object of the suppression of exchange restrictions can be achieved only when the dangers to currency arising from the problem of transfers are banished and confidence is restored.

ii) *Long-term debts:* In the case of those long-term debts, the burden of which has been so aggravated by the present level of prices as to be incompatible with the equilibrium of the balance of payments, agreements should be concluded between debtors and the bondholders. Nevertheless, it is essential for this problem, as for the problem of short-term debts, that a satisfactory solution should be reached if the equilibrium of the balance of payments is to be secured and normal conditions restored.

Such a solution must be sought between the interested parties working together. In certain cases, bondholders have already formed associations; in others, it might be useful for such groups to be formed. Moreover, the associations of different countries should keep in touch with each other. The issue houses should be in a position to lend their good offices in this connection to the bondholders.

In order to facilitate, where necessary, direct agreements between debtors and creditors, a list of persons of recognised standing and competence might be drawn up whose mediation would be open to the parties concerned.

We should like to point out that, in this sphere also, there is no uniform solution for all cases.

3. Capital Movements

The resumption of the movement of capital throughout the world—in other words, the re-establishment of international financing—should be effected through the normal credit channels. The creation of a special credit institution may be expected to promote this resumption. There is no doubt that, as soon as the world situation again becomes normal, credit will begin to operate as in the past. It will be asked for, granted or refused by the usual means. It should be noted that available credit has not disappeared. On the contrary, there is an abundant supply, but, for the reasons mentioned above, it is not being used. In view of past experience it would, however, be desirable to encourage the exchange of information as to the volume and movement of short-term credits.

At the same time, the resumption of lending may prove to be slow if no organised international action is taken to stimulate it. A number of projects have been discussed on various occasions.

Among the suggestions brought to the committee's notice is the establishment of a Monetary Normalisation Fund, which was contemplated at the Stresa Conference.

It might, in fact, happen that, after all the foregoing recommendations had been applied, the responsible public authorities might still be reluctant to re-establish the freedom of exchange transactions, in which case even a moderate amount of assistance from outside might help to restore their confidence and that of the public as well.

In view of the fact that the object of the establishment of such a fund is to facilitate monetary normalisation, the Bank for International Settlements would appear to be the most appropriate body to administer this fund, since it is desirable to avoid any political influence in its administration.

This idea of special assistance proving necessary to restart the financial machine, which has been at a standstill for so long, has been further developed in the course of our deliberations. The suggestion has been made that help might be given by means of the establishment of an international credit institute, which would derive its funds either from the banks of issue or from private sources, the support of the governments being provided in both cases, as would also be necessary in the case of the Monetary Normalisation Fund.

Obviously, an institution of this kind—the object of which would be to set in motion capital which is at present lying idle—should grant new credits only under sound conditions and subject to strict supervision with a view to preventing any inflation. It should not refund the old credits ("frozen" credits) referred to above. It is also obvious that this institute should be free from any political influence, and it might be affiliated to or administered by the Bank for International Settlements. If this idea meets with the approval of the governments, we suggest that the question should be gone into more fully.

As another method of encouraging capital movements, a programme of public works on an international scale has been submitted to the commission. We feel that it is not probable that public works can be internationally financed in the immediate future to any considerable extent. The last year has brought out to an unprecedented degree the dangers of over-borrowing and the exchange difficulties which may arise in connection with effecting the service of foreign loans. Quite apart from this, governments are now receiving so many demands which they have to refuse, and, moreover, have to retrench in so many directions, that they must consider carefully before embarking upon new budgetary commitments of this nature.

We recognise, however, that, should any government in a lending country desire to promote the chances of obtaining capital for this purpose by giving some form of guarantee, it is obvious that the commencement of the works that have been proposed would be expedited thereby, at a moment when even the best projects find it difficult to receive the requisite funds. It goes without saying, especially in existing conditions, that sound financial principles demand that only such public works should be financed as afford adequate assurance of being productive of the domestic and foreign currency necessary for the service of the capital charges.

APPENDIX B

JOINT STATEMENTS ON WASHINGTON CONSULTATIONS

I. AMERICAN-BRITISH STATEMENT[1]

As stated yesterday, our discussions on the questions facing the World Conference were not designed to result in definitive agreements, which must be left to the conference itself. But they showed that our two governments were looking with a like purpose and a close similarity of method at the main objectives of the conference, and were impressed by the vital necessity of assuring international agreements for their realization in the interests of the peoples of all countries. The practical measures which are required for their realization were analysed and explored. The necessity for an increase in the general level of commodity prices was recognised as primary and fundamental. To this end simultaneous action needs to be taken both in the economic and in the monetary field. Commercial policies have to be set to a new orientation. There should be a constructive effort to moderate the network of restrictions of all sorts by which commerce is at present hampered, such as excessive tariffs, quotas, exchange restrictions, etc. Central banks should by concerted action provide an adequate expansion of credit and every means should be used to get the credit thus created into circulation. Enterprise must be stimulated by creating conditions favorable to business recovery and governments can contribute by the development of appropriate programs of capital expenditure. The ultimate re-establishment of equilibrium in the international exchanges should also be contemplated. We must when circumstances permit re-establish an international monetary standard which will operate successfully without depressing prices and avoid the repetition of the mistakes which have produced such disastrous results in the past. In this connection the question of silver, which is of such importance in trade with the Orient, was

[1] Issued April 26, 1933 by President Roosevelt and Prime Minister MacDonald.

discussed and proposals were tentatively suggested for the improvement of its status.

These questions are all interrelated and cannot be settled by any individual country acting by itself. The achievement of sound and lasting world recovery depends on co-ordinatii domestic remedies and supplementing them by concurrent and simultaneous action in the international field. The proposals examined will be discussed with the representatives of the other nations who have been invited to Washington with a view to securing the fullest possible measure of common understanding before the conference meets. It is the hope of both governments that it may be possible to convene the conference for June.

We have in these talks found a reassurance of unity of purpose and method. They have given a fresh impetus to the solution of the problems that weigh so heavily upon the most stable, industrious and deserving men and women of the world—the human foundation of our civilization whose hard lot it is our common object to alleviate.

II. AMERICAN-FRENCH STATEMENT[2]

Our conversations had as their object and as their result as complete an understanding as possible between our two countries in regard to our common problems, the conclusion of definite agreements being reserved for the forthcoming World Monetary and Economic Conference.

At no moment has understanding been more necessary between France and the United States for the maintenance of peace, for progressive and simultaneous economic disarmament of the world, and for the restoration of stable monetary conditions in an atmosphere of general security.

We have noted with deep satisfaction that our two governments are looking with like purpose at the main problems of the world and the objectives of the Economic Conference.

The government of the United States and the government of France have been able already to announce their full agreement in regard to the necessity of a prompt meeting of the conference, the object of which must be to bring about a rapid revival of

[2] Issued April 28, 1933 by President Roosevelt and M. Herriot. Translated from the official French text.

world activity and the raising of world prices by diminishing all sorts of impediments to international commerce such as tariffs, quotas, and exchange restrictions, and by the re-establishment of a normal financial and monetary situation.

We have examined more particularly the conditions under which commercial policy should henceforth develop in order to promote rather than restrict the movement of goods. We have studied monetary problems and the different methods possible for a co-ordination of central bank policy; the remedies which might be brought forward to attack the menacing problem of unemployment and the stagnation of business by the execution of programs of public works to be carried out by different governments by such methods as are within their means; the effects of the depression on silver and the different methods proposed to improve its status.

The questions which confront the world at this time are, in our opinion, for the most part closely linked together. They constitute the elements of a single problem, a sane and durable solution of which must be sought in collaboration which would render complete, on an international scale, indispensable domestic efforts.

The suffering of millions of workers throughout the world renders imperative the earliest possible consummation of such collaboration, so happily begun here.

In conclusion, our conversations, which have been so frank and cordial, have made it possible for us to ascertain the determination of our countries to enter into such collaboration and to seek to extend it to other nations with a view to ensuring for all peoples an opportunity to work in conditions of real peace.

III. AMERICAN-ITALIAN STATEMENT[3]

At the close of our conversations we note with profound satisfaction the close similarity of our views on the questions which are harassing the world today. The world faces a crisis of the first magnitude. If normal life is to be resumed, the World Economic Conference must be made a success. It must not only meet soon, but come to its conclusions quickly. The task is so complex and difficult that unless it is approached by all nations

[3] Issued May 6, 1933 by President Roosevelt and Signor Jung.

with the fullest and sincerest desire to arrive at a result, the conference cannot succeed. But the other course before the world is clearly an increase in economic warfare and all nations must co-operate in attempting to avoid this alternative.

We agree that political tranquillity is essential for economic stability; that economic disarmament can take place only in a world in which military disarmament is possible.

A truce in the field of tariffs and other obstacles to international trade is essential if the conference is to undertake its labors with any hope of success. We are in agreement that a fixed measure of exchange values must be re-established in the world and we believe that this measure must be gold.

The entire problem of raising world prices and restoring the opportunity to work to the men and women who today wish to work and can find no employment is a unit. It must be attacked as a unit. Along with the measures which must be taken to restore normal conditions in the financial and monetary field, and stability in international exchanges must go hand in hand measures for removing the obstacles to the flow of international commerce.

In the period immediately before us, governments must employ such means as are at their disposal to relieve the unemployed by public works, and these efforts of individual governments will achieve their fullest effect if they can be made a part of a synchronized international program. Similarly, the central banks of the various nations should by concerted action attempt to provide such adequate expansion of credit as may be necessary to support constructive work, avoiding as much as possible the use of credit for illegitimate speculative purposes.

We have found ourselves in the closest agreement on many other measures to re-establish the economic life of the world and we are both determined to approach the problems of the World Economic Conference with the firmest resolve to bring its labors to success.

APPENDIX C

AMERICAN DECLARATIONS OF POLICY AT THE LONDON CONFERENCE

I. DRAFT RESOLUTION ON CREDIT AND PRICES[1]

WHEREAS, industry and trade in nearly all the major countries of the world have fallen to unprecedently low levels, and

WHEREAS, as a consequence thereof, millions of people throughout the world have been thrown out of employment and unwillingly have become an ever increasing burden upon those who still have employment, and

WHEREAS, the emergency is of such a nature as to demand that all nations and all peoples co-operate to the fullest possible extent in combating the depression by all available means and in close consultation and harmony with each other, and

WHEREAS, abundant credit and wise encouragement of private enterprise through government expenditure are essential in bringing about an improvement in prices and an increase of business activity, and

WHEREAS, such government expenditure shall not necessarily be included in the budget for recurring expenses but may properly be financed by borrowing, provided that the service of government debt so incurred is taken care of in a balanced budget for recurring expenses.

NOW THEREFORE BE IT RESOLVED, that all the nations participating in this conference agree

a) That a close co-operation toward these ends between governments and between their respective central banks should be undertaken;

b) That a primary step in such co-operation should be the carrying out of a policy of making credit abundantly and readily available to sound enterprise; this may be done by open market operations, where consistent with national policy, or by such other means as may suit the particular requirements of an individual market; and

c) That an acceleration of the process of recovery should be sought by means of a synchronized program of governmental expenditure in the different countries along parallel lines, designed to stimulate the natural

---

[1] Introduced June 22 by the American delegation to the conference.

sources of employment, to re-start the wheels of industry and commerce, and to restore the willingness of the individual again to assume the normal risks of trade without which any recovery is impossible.

It is not the sense of this resolution that all nations should agree necessarily to attack the problem in the same way, but rather that the efforts already being made by many nations should be co-ordinated, and that other nations should be stimulated to make similar efforts.

It should be borne in mind that in the development of such a program care must be exercised lest the cost of a particular kind of work undertaken be inordinately increased whether on the part of suppliers, landowners or wage earners particularly concerned.

AND BE IT FURTHER RESOLVED,

a) That the issue banks of the various nations be requested to send at once to London a representative or representatives for the purpose of immediate consultation with each other, and

b) That a committee be appointed by this conference to study the various methods of governmental expenditure which have been in use or under consideration by the various nations, with a view towards making a report to be sent to each of the nations for its guidance in working out its own program in the future.

II. DRAFT RESOLUTION ON RESTORATION OF THE GOLD STANDARD[2]

WHEREAS, confusion now exists in the field of international exchange, and

WHEREAS, it is essential to world recovery that an international monetary standard should be re-established.

NOW THEREFORE, BE IT RESOLVED that all the nations participating in this conference agree

a) That it is in the interests of all concerned that stability in the international monetary field be attained as quickly as practicable;

b) That gold should be re-established as the international measure of exchange values;

c) That the use of gold should be confined to its employment as cover for circulation and as a medium of settling international balances of payment. This means that gold, either in coin or bullion, will be withdrawn from circulation;

d) That in order to improve the workings of a future gold standard

---

[2] Introduced June 19 by Senator Key Pittman in the name of the American delegation to the conference.

a uniform legal minimum gold cover for the currencies of the various countries which shall adopt the gold standard shall be established, and that this legal minimum reserve shall be lower than the average of the present reserve requirements;

e) That the central banks of the various nations be requested to meet at once in order to consider the adoption of such a uniform minimum reserve ratio and that a metal cover of 25 per cent be recommended for their consideration,

AND FURTHER, WHEREAS, silver constitutes an important medium of both international and domestic exchange for a large proportion of the world's population, and

WHEREAS, the value of this purchasing medium has been impaired by governmental action in the past, and

WHEREAS, it is necessary that the confidence of the East should be restored in its purchasing medium, which can only be done if the price of silver is restored to equilibrium with commodity price levels,

NOW THEREFORE BE IT RESOLVED *that*

a) An agreement be sought between the chief silver producing countries and those countries which are large holders or users of silver to limit arbitrary sales upon the world market;

b) That all nations agree to prevent further debasement of their subsidiary silver coinages;

c) That all the nations agree to remonetize their subsidiary coinages up to a fineness of at least 800 when, as and if consistent with their respective national budget problems; and

d) That it be recommended to the central banks that they agree that 80 per cent of their metal cover shall be in gold and 20 per cent shall be optionally in gold or in silver, provided that silver is obtainable at or below a price to be agreed upon as corresponding to the general commodity price level; and that the governments agree to modify their respective laws to this effect.

III. OFFICIAL STATEMENT RELATIVE TO PRESIDENT ROOSEVELT'S MESSAGE TO THE CONFERENCE[3]

The President has made it clear that he saw no utility at the present time in temporary stabilisation between the currencies of countries whose needs and policies are not necessarily the same. Such stabilisation would be artificial and unreal and might hamper individual countries in realising policies essential to their domestic problem. He urged the conference to seek considera-

[3] Transmitted July 5 by the American delegation to the conference.

tion of its fundamental task of facilitating policies by the different nations directly, not to temporary expedients, but to mitigating and, if possible, remedying the harassing evils of the present economic situation. In the hope that the United States may be of help to the conference, to whose success and friendly co-operation the President continues to attach the greatest importance, it may be useful that we should develop this thought somewhat more fully.

The revaluation of the dollar in terms of American commodities is an end from which the government and the people of the United States cannot be diverted. We wish to make this perfectly clear: we are interested in American commodity prices. What is to be the value of the dollar in terms of foreign currencies is not and cannot be our immediate concern. The exchange value of the dollar will ultimately depend upon the success of other nations in raising the prices of their own commodities in terms of their national moneys and cannot be determined in advance of our knowledge of such fact. There is nothing in our policy inimical to the interest of any other country and we are confident that no other country would seek to embarrass us in the attainment of economic ends required for our economic health.

When the currencies of those great nations of the Continent of Europe—France, Italy, and Belgium—depreciated over a period of years, there was no criticism from the United States, nor did we criticise their ultimate devaluation. And when Great Britain and the Scandinavian countries went off the gold standard there was only sympathetic understanding in the United States. Great Britain has been off the gold standard for nearly a year and three-quarters and the United States has been off for less than three months. Nevertheless, we are glad to be able to associate ourselves with the statement of British policy made on July 4th in the House of Commons by the Financial Secretary to the Treasury, when, speaking in the name of the Chancellor of the Exchequer, he said:

"My right hon. friend has on a number of occasions expressed the view of His Majesty's Government that, although a return to the gold standard might be our ultimate objective when proper conditions were assured, we must reserve completely liberty to choose both our own time and parity. He does not think he can usefully add anything to that statement now."

If there are countries where prices and costs are already in actual equilibrium we do not regard it to be the task of the conference, as it certainly is not the purpose of the American government, to persuade or compel them to pursue policies contrary to their own conception of their own interests.

It is not sufficient to escape from the present evils. But it is our duty to consider together how to avoid their recurrence in the future. The first task is to restore prices to a level at which industry, and above all agriculture, can function profitably and efficiently. The second task is to preserve the stability of this adjustment once achieved. The part which gold and silver should play after adjustment has been secured would seem a further subject suitable for consideration by the conference.

We conceive therefore that the great problems which justify the assembling of the nations are as present today and as deserving of exploration as was the case a few weeks ago; and we find it difficult to conceive that the view which it has been our obvious duty to take on the minor issue of temporary stabilisation can in any way diminish the advisability of such discussion.

BRITISH DECLARATION OF POLICY AT THE LONDON CONFERENCE[1]

I should like to emphasise our view that there is a close connection between the monetary, financial and economic aspects of our problem, and that action must be taken simultaneously in all these spheres.

This is well illustrated by the first proposition which I should like to submit to you, namely, that it is essential to bring about a recovery in the world level of wholesale commodity prices sufficient to yield an economic return to the producers of primary commodities and to restore equilibrium between costs and prices of production, generally. It is clear that the present lack of equilibrium between prices and costs can only be remedied *either* by a further drastic reduction of wages and other costs and by widespread bankruptcies, *or* by a sufficient recovery in the level of wholesale prices.

In the opinion of the United Kingdom delegation, an attempt to obtain equilibrium by further large reductions of cost would be attended by intolerable suffering and holds out no hope of success. No doubt it would be possible to restore equilibrium between prices and costs by reducing costs if only prices would remain steady. Under present conditions that does not happen, but, on the contrary, an all-round reduction in costs produces further deflationary effects on prices, so that costs and prices chase one another downwards without ever getting to equilibrium. Moreover, there is one all-important entity in each country which finds it particularly difficult to reduce its own costs; I mean the central government. Every finance minister in the world knows only too well how tremendously resistant public expenditure is to reduction, if only for the reason that so many of its obligations are fixed in terms of money. A policy of reducing costs and prices has the inevitable effect of very greatly reducing the national

[1] Excerpts from speech delivered at the conference June 14 by the British Chancellor of the Exchequer.

income, with the consequence that, in order to balance its accounts, the government must take by taxation a larger and larger proportion of the income of the country. Sooner or later, usually sooner, this process is found to be intolerable, and countries bent on securing heavy reductions in costs and prices find that they have merely secured an unbalanced budget for which no practical cure can be found. In the view of the British delegation, therefore, a solution of our present difficulties must be found by means of a recovery in the price level.

To bring about a recovery in prices, action in various spheres will be necessary. The final settlement of reparations and war debts is not within the scope of this conference, but such a settlement is essential if the measures taken in other fields are to be effective.

As regards these, a number of reforms are required in the financial sphere; for example, the abrogation of exchange controls and the resumption of international lending; and also in the economic sphere, such as the co-ordination of production and marketing, the removal of prohibitions and similar trade barriers, and the reduction of excessive tariffs in order to permit a normal flow of international trade. I will refer to these later.

But, in order to attain the object of a recovery in prices, action is also necessary in the monetary sphere. The fundamental monetary condition of the recovery of prices is that credit should be made available by a policy of cheap money and that such credit should be actively employed. This, together with the revival of business confidence, must form the indispensable background of trade recovery.

The control of monetary policy is largely in the hands of the central banks and the practical steps to give effect to the requisite monetary policy have to be taken by them, and in particular by those of the most important financial centres. These central banks should therefore undertake to co-operate with a view to securing the monetary conditions required for a rise in prices. In order that their action may have the desired effect, it is necessary that the policy of cheap and plentiful money should be clearly announced and vigorously pursued. Particularly, the wider extension of what is known as "open market operations" by central banks should, in our view, be developed.

Experience in recent months has shown that cheap money in itself may not be enough to achieve the desired end rapidly unless means are taken to ensure that the credit made available is actively employed. This in turn depends upon the establishment of a sense of security and confidence in the public, and so again it is seen how inextricably finance and politics are intermingled.

The question whether governments can effectively assist in this matter by schemes of government capital expenditure will also require consideration. The United Kingdom delegation will be very ready to examine with other delegations how far employment can be stimulated by such action. In our view, however, it would be a mistake to attempt to lay down any rigidly uniform policy for different countries on this point. The extent to which employment can be stimulated by government capital expenditure necessarily depends upon the circumstances of each country, and, in particular, upon the extent to which opportunities are still open for self-supporting schemes, which in turn must depend partly upon the extent to which in each country schemes have already been promoted in the past. Each government must therefore determine, in the light of the situation in its own country, the size and nature of any further programme which it can wisely promote, and the method by which it should be financed.

A further matter which falls within the monetary sphere concerns the values of the principal currencies of the world in relation to each other. As the greatest international traders in the world, we fully recognise the great importance to international trade of stability of exchange rates. In our opinion, the attainment of this object must necessarily be attempted in two stages. The immediate objective should be to secure approximate stability between the currencies of the principal countries of the world in order that trade may not be hampered by violent and unpredictable fluctuations of what I may call the basic currencies. This end will be achieved in so far as the principal countries use their resources in order to counteract fluctuations in the value of their currency caused by temporary movements of capital rather than by fundamental economic factors.

This first stage should be dealt with immediately. As regards the second stage, the United Kingdom delegation endorse the view that the ultimate aim of monetary policy should be the restoration of a satisfactory international standard, and there is no doubt that a gold standard seems to be generally acceptable. The time and the exchange parity at which a return to gold could safely be made, must, as was pointed out in the Annotated Agenda prepared by the Preparatory Commission, fall to be determined by the proper authorities in each country separately, but in order that all countries may work harmoniously towards the same goal I have no doubt that the conference would wish me to state, in as positive and concrete terms as possible, the conditions under which the United Kingdom would feel justified in returning to the gold standard.

One of these conditions is a rise in the general level of the wholesale prices of commodities sufficient to restore equilibrium between prices and costs.

A second condition is an adjustment of the factors which caused the breakdown of the gold standard in the past and which, if not corrected, would inevitably lead to a repetition of the process in the future. These factors include, of course, the disturbances due to reparations and war debt payments, and the obstacles to international trade caused by excessive tariffs, exchange restrictions, and other abnormal impediments to the flow of commerce.

A third condition is that the gold standard shall in the future be so administered that wide fluctuations in the purchasing power of gold (in so far as they arise from monetary causes) will be to the greatest possible extent prevented. Without entering in detail into the question of the requisite reforms in the working of the gold standard (in regard to which I hope that a substantial measure of international agreement will be found to exist) I will only mention three which seem to us essential, namely the withdrawal of gold from internal circulation and its use only for settlement of international balances; the reduction in the legal minimum proportions of gold which central banks are required to hold in their reserves; and a closer permanent co-operation between central banks.

REPORT OF THE MONETARY AND FINANCIAL COMMISSION OF THE LONDON CONFERENCE[1]

I. REPORT BY H. E. M. GEORGES BONNET (FRANCE)

1. The Monetary and Financial Commission began work under the presidency of Governor Cox on June 16th. It decided at its first meeting to adopt the Draft Annotated Agenda drawn up by the Prepartory Commission of Experts as the basis of its programme.

With a view to systematic study of its programme, the commission divided into two sub-commissions. The first on "immediate measures for financial reconstruction," with H. E. M. G. Jung as president, had the following subjects on its agenda:

Credit policy;
Price levels;
Limitation of monetary fluctuations;
Exchange control;
Indebtedness;
Resumption of international lending.

The second sub-commission on "permanent measures for the re-establishment of an international monetary standard," with Dr. Kienböck as president, was charged with the study of the following points:

Functions of central banks;
Co-ordination of their policies;
Silver;
Gold exchange standard and other means of economising gold;
Distribution of monetary reserves.

All the countries represented at the conference were entitled to take part in the work of the two sub-commissions, and representatives of the Financial Committee of the League of Nations and the President of the Bank for International Settlements were also invited to participate.

[1] League of Nations Document No. C. 435. M. 220. 1933. II. [Conf. M.E. 22(1)].

Further, each of the two sub-commissions entrusted the study of certain special problems and the drawing up of draft resolutions to small sub-committees as circumstances required.

2. A number of meetings were devoted by each of the sub-commissions to a detailed exchange of views on the general aspects of the questions forming their programme as outlined above. This initial work brought to light the inter-dependence of the majority of the problems involved, and the necessity for first settling certain fundamental questions which might pave the way to the agreements which it was the function of the sub-commissions to seek. It was, however, agreed after a full exchange of views that solutions of these fundamental problems on an international basis were for the moment impossible, and that in these circumstances it was better to postpone their discussion. The sub-commissions accordingly decided to concentrate on those points the discussion of which was likely to lead to immediate results, and in agreement with the bureau of the conference they modified their programme accordingly.

3. In these circumstances, they achieved the results which you will find embodied in the reports they have prepared. These reports have been adopted by the Monetary and Financial Commission and I, in my turn, have the honour to submit them to you for your approval (see Annexes 1 and 2).

4. The Sub-Commission I unanimously adopted the text of a resolution relating to indebtedness submitted to it by the drafting committee set up for the purpose. The adoption of this resolution was accompanied by interpretative explanations from the delegations of the Argentine Republic and the Dominican Republic.

The Sub-Commission I brings its report to a close with the statement that the discussion of the other subjects on the agenda did not proceed far enough to do more than outline the main problems to be solved. It adds that it will, however, be prepared to resume its task at a later stage.

5. The Sub-Commission II unanimously adopted the following five resolutions:

a) A resolution relating to the return to monetary stability, the adoption of gold as an international monetary standard, its use for monetary requirements and the legal cover of central banks.

The Bulgarian delegation made a reservation with regard to this resolution.

b) A resolution relating to the creation of central banks.

c) A resolution relating to the need for close and continuous co-operation between central banks and to the part which might be played by the Bank for International Settlements in this connection.

d) A resolution relating to the adaptation of the central banks of certain agricultural countries to the special economic conditions of those countries.

The Yugoslav delegation entered a reservation to this resolution.

e) A resolution relating to silver, the adoption of which was accompanied by explanations from the Mexican delegation and an interpretation by the French delegation.

Sub-Commission II further mentions in its report the communication made to it by one of its sub-committees regarding the general principles of the monetary policy of central banks. All the governments represented on the sub-committee approved these principles, except the United States delegation, which considered discussion of the question at this time premature, it being understand that the Federal Reserve Banks would be glad to confer at an opportune time with other central banks on questions of this character to the extent that they were compatible with national policies.

With regard to the part of its agenda dealing with the gold exchange standard and other methods of economising gold, and the distribution of monetary reserves, Sub-Commission II was not able to complete its report during the present session.

It took note, however, of a recommendation made to it by the sub-committee entrusted with the study of these questions, to the effect that the Bank for International Settlements would examine the problem of the gold exchange standard as soon as possible and would, in particular, consider how far it might be found possible to avoid some of the drawbacks which this system has revealed in the past. The conference will certainly wish to endorse this recommendation.

6. The conference will not fail to appreciate the importance of the results already obtained. It is, I think, reasonable to suppose that, when the future work of the Monetary and Financial Commission has led to the conclusion of wider agreements, these agreements will embody the principles which the resolutions adopted record.

Before concluding my report, I should like to draw the attention of the conference to the extreme importance of the discussions which have taken place at the meetings of your Monetary and Financial Commission and of its various organs of enquiry and which could not be faithfully reflected in the resolutions submitted to you. The questions reserved for further study also gave rise to exhaustive discussions in which all those taking part were inspired by a sense of the grave nature of the task devolving upon this conference and by a wish to reach solutions which would justify the hopes the whole world has set upon it. If your commission has not on this occasion solved all the problems submitted to it, it feels sure that a way will soon be found to reconcile views which, differing as regards means, are identical as regards the ultimate aims. On the resumption of the general discussions, which the bureau will be empowered to arrange for when the time comes, the real value of the substantial work done by your Monetary and Financial Commission at this first session will become fully apparent.

II. ANNEXES

Annex I

Report of Sub-Commission I: Immediate Measures for Financial Reconstruction

Chairman: H. E. M. Guido Jung (Italy)

Following the appointment of the Sub-Commission on Immediate Measures for Financial Reconstruction by the Monetary and Financial Commission to consider the following questions —credit policy, price levels, limitation of currency fluctuations, exchange controls, problems of indebtedness, resumption of lending—the first meeting of your sub-commission was held on June 19th and five public sessions were held between June 19th and 21st, in which a general discussion took place on the questions of credit policy and price levels. A draft resolution was submitted by the United Kingdom delegation and a further resolution was proposed by the United States delegation.

Four public sessions followed between June 22nd and 27th, in which a general discussion took place on the problems of indebtedness. Draft resolutions were submitted by the Hungarian and Roumanian delegations.

On June 27th, it was decided to appoint a sub-committee to make concrete proposals relating to the procedure to be adopted.

This sub-committee met the same day and decided to appoint two drafting committees to prepare resolutions, the first on the question of credit policy and the second on the problems of indebtedness.

The first drafting committee met on June 28th, and discussed a paper submitted by the United Kingdom delegation. However, the working of this committee was deferred in view of certain events affecting the possibility of reaching, for the time being, full agreement on the terms of resolutions on the subject.

The general policy was reviewed by the bureau of the conference at its meeting on July 6th, when it requested each sub-commission to draw up as soon as possible a list of questions which, in the circumstances, could be usefully studied.

Your sub-commission held two public sessions on July 7th in connection with this request, and a proposal of the United Kingdom delegation that all the items on the agenda should be included in the list to be submitted to the bureau was adopted by 25 votes to 15, with one abstention; 23 delegations were not present. Three of these subsequently expressed their adherence to the United Kingdom proposal.

On July 11th, the bureau of the conference decided to recommend that your sub-commission should proceed for the time being with the discussion on the problems of indebtedness. This task was confided to the second drafting committee appointed on June 27th, which held five private meetings between July 12th and 18th, and reported through the Chancellor of the Exchequer on July 20th to your sub-commission the following resolution, which was unanimously adopted:

1. The service of external debts is in different degrees an important item among the liabilities in the balance of payments of many countries and can only be assured if the debtor country can procure the necessary resources. The facility with which such resources can be procured in the present and in the future may depend on the revival of economic activity and credit. It would be assisted by a return to a reasonable degree of freedom in the movement of goods and services and the creditor countries in particular should co-operate to this end. It will also depend on the economic and financial policy adopted by the debtor country. In present conditions a solution of the problem of indebtedness may in certain cases

be necessary for the re-stablishment of equilbrium. It should not, however, be dealt with in such a way as to impair credit.

2. The conditions in the debtor countries vary considerably and it is not possible to lay down a uniform treatment applicable to all cases. But debtors should make every possible effort to meet the service of their debts and to fulfill their contracts.

It is indispensable, indeed, for the restoration of credit that contracts should be respected in the absence of modifications agreed between the parties concerned.

3. When arrangements are recognised to be necessary care should be taken by all concerned to secure the maintenance of confidence. They should, therefore, be limited to those cases where they are unavoidable, be made directly between debtors and creditors and be based on the debtor's ability to pay. As regards state loans, it is in the interest of the creditors themselves to conclude arrangements of such a nature as will permit the adoption at the same time of a programme of economic and financial restoration by the debtor countries and its effective application.

4. It is desirable that in each of the countries concerned there should exist organisations in a position to represent the several classes of creditors in respect of foreign loans, including, in suitable cases, short as well as long term loans, and that such organizations should maintain such contact with one another as may be necessary to facilitate their proceedings. The commission therefore recommends to the governments of these countries that they should encourage the creation of and contact between organisations of this kind where they do not already exist, at such times and in such measure as action can in their view be usefully applied.

5. The question of inter-governmental debts lies entirely outside the field of discussion of this conference.

The discussion of the other subjects on the agenda did not proceed far enough to do more than outline the main problems to be solved. Your sub-commission will however be prepared to resume in order that its task can be completed at a later stage.

Annex II

Report of Sub-Commission II: Permanent Measures for the Re-establishment of an International Monetary Standard

Chairman: Dr. V. Kienböck (Austria)

1. On June 19th, the Monetary and Financial Commission decided to divide its work between two sub-commissions. Sub-Commission II, with which this report deals, was set up to consider permanent measures for the re-establishment of an international monetary standard. The agenda proposed for the sub-commission was:

The functions of central banks;
The co-ordination of their policies;
Monetary reserves;
Silver.

2. All the delegations at the conference were invited to send representatives to the sub-commission. The representatives of the Financial Committee of the League of Nations and the President of the Bank for International Settlements were also invited to co-operate in its work.

Dr. V. Kienböck (Austria) was appointed president of the sub-commission.

3. At its first meeting (June 19th) the sub-commission took as the basis of its discussions a draft resolution submitted by the United States delegation, the second part of a proposal submitted by the Swiss delegation to Sub-Commission I, and the second part of proposals submitted by the Roumanian delegation on behalf of the Bulgarian, Latvian, Polish, Roumanian, Czechoslovak and Yugoslav delegations. It was decided to set up two sub-committees, one to deal with the question of silver and the second to deal with the technical monetary problems connected with the working of the gold standard. Senator Pittman presided over the former and Dr. Kienböck, and in his absence Mr. Postmus, over the latter.

4. At its second meeting on June 20th, the sub-commission unanimously adopted the following resolutions:

I. (a) That it is in the interests of all concerned that stability in the international monetary field be attained as quickly as practicable;

b) That gold should be re-established as the international measure of exchange values, time and parity being for each country to determine.

5. After private discussions and conversations among the delegations primarily concerned, the sub-commission, on July 20th, on the recommendation of the Sub-Committee on Silver, unanimously adopted the following draft resolution which was based on a draft submitted by the United States delegation:

Be it resolved to recommend to all the governments parties to this conference

V. (a) That an agreement be sought between the chief silver producing countries and those countries which are the largest holders or users of silver, with a view to mitigating fluctuations in the price of silver; and that the other nations not parties to such agreement should refrain from measures which could appreciably affect the silver market;

b) That governments parties to this conference shall refrain from new legislative measures which would involve further debasement of their silver coinage below a fineness of 800/1000;

c) That they shall substitute silver coins for low value paper currency in so far as the budgetary and local conditions of each country will permit;

d) That all of the provisions of this resolution are subject to the following exceptions and limitations:

The requirements of such provisions shall lapse on April 1, 1934, if the agreement recommended in paragraph (a) does not come into force by that date, and in no case shall extend beyond January 1st, 1938;

Governments may take any action relative to their silver coinage that they may deem necessary to prevent the flight or destruction of their silver coinage by reason of a rise in the bullion price of silver content of their coin above the nominal or parity value of such silver coin.

6. The Sub-Committee on Technical Monetary Problems began its work on June 21st, with a consideration of monetary gold reserves, taking as the basis of its discussion clauses (c), (d) and (e) of the draft resolution presented by the United States delegation. Mr. Fraser, president of the Bank for International Settlements, was appointed *rapporteur*.

7. At the fourth meeting of the sub-commission held on June 28th, the following resolutions were presented:

I. (c) That under modern conditions monetary gold is required not for internal circulation but as a reserve against central bank liabilities and primarily to meet external demands for payments caused by some disequilibrium on the foreign account. It is consequently undesirable to put gold coins or gold certificates into internal circulation.

d) That in order to improve the working of a future gold standard greater elasticity should be given to central bank legal cover provisions; for instance, in so far as the system of percentage gold cover is applied a minimum ratio of not more than twenty-five per cent should be considered as sufficient; similar elasticity should be achieved by appropriate measures where other systems are applied. However, such changes must not be taken as an excuse for unduly building up a larger superstructure of notes and credits; in other words the effect of this resolution should be to increase the free reserve of central banks and thereby to strengthen their position.

These resolutions were unanimously adopted by the sub-commission with an amendment proposed by the Egyptian delegation that the word "minimum" should be inserted before "ratio" in draft resolution (d). The Bulgarian delegation while accepting the draft resolution (c) made the reservation that in present conditions its government was unable to use its central bank's gold reserves to meet the disequilibrium on the foreign account because such a step would prove seriously prejudicial to public confidence in the note circulation.

The German delegation having proposed to insert the word "temporary" before "disequilibrium" in draft resolution (c), in order to make it clear that the resolution did not favour the use of central bank gold reserves to meet a permanent disequilibrium in the balance of payments, withdrew its proposal upon the *rapporteur* explaining that the resolution did not mean that central banks of countries with a permanent deficit in their balance of accounts would have to be deprived of the whole of the gold in their possession and so compromise the internal note circulation.

8. The Sub-Committee on Technical Monetary Problems resumed consideration of the remaining items of its agenda on June 29th, dealing with co-operation among central banks. In this connection it took into consideration a proposal by the Roumanian delegation concerning the adaptation of the central banks of agricultural countries to the special conditions of those countries.

9. On July 11th, the bureau of the conference adopted a resolution that—

The Monetary and Financial Sub-Commission II should take up the resolutions, already adopted by its sub-committees, on central banking co-operation and on the creation of central banks in certain countries where they do not now exist, and should pursue, through its sub-committees, the examination of the question of silver and any other subject on its agenda which may by general agreement be considered suitable for discussion.

10. In pursuance of the bureau's resolution, the sub-commission met on July 14th, and unanimously adopted the three following resolutions:

II. The conference considers it to be essential, in order to provide an international gold standard with the necessary mechanism for satisfactory working, that independent central banks, with the requisite powers and freedom to carry out an appropriate currency and credit policy, should be created in such developed countries as have not at present an adequate central banking institution.

III. The conference wish to reaffirm the declarations of previous conferences with regard to the great utility of close and continuous co-operation between central banks. The Bank for International Settlements should play an increasingly important part not only by improving contact, but also as an instrument for common action.

IV. The sub-committee has taken note of the suggestions of the Roumanian delegation with a view to securing the adaptation of the central banks of certain agricultural countries to the special economic conditions of these countries and of the views expressed in the discussion thereof. The sub-committee feels that the local conditions in each country will to a very large extent determine the solutions to be adopted in this matter and suggests that if any countries desire advice on these questions in view of their technical character they might appropriately be considered by the international organisations specially competent to advise on these matters.

The Yugoslav delegation made a declaration accepting resolution IV, at the same time stating that the legal minimum cover should not be diminished below the percentage recommended by the sub-commission in resolution I (d).

11. The sub-commission held its final meeting on monetary problems on July 20th. The following resolution was communicated to it:

The sub-committee approves the annexed statement of general principles of central banks monetary policy which was laid before it.

1) The proper functioning of the gold standard requires in the first place the adoption by each individual central bank of a policy designed to maintain a fundamental equilibrium in the balance of payments of its country. Gold movements which reflect a lack of such an equilibrium constitute therefore an essential factor in determining central bank policy.

2) Gold movements so far as they seem to be of a more permanent character should normally not be prevented from making their influence felt both in the country losing gold and in the country receiving gold.

3) While gold should be allowed freely to flow out of and into the countries concerned, central banks should always be prepared to buy gold at a publicly announced fixed price expressed in their currency, and to sell gold at a publicly announced fixed price, expressed in their currency, the latter at least when exchange rates reach gold points.

4) Central banks should obtain from their markets the fullest possible information concerning the demands that might be made upon their reserves.

5) Since as already stated under (1) the proper functioning of the gold standard requires in the first place the adoption by each individual central bank of a policy designed to maintain a fundamental equilibrium in the balance of payments of its country, the discretion of each central bank in regulating the working of the gold standard in its own country should remain unimpaired. Central banks should, however, recognise that in addition to their national task they have also to fulfil a task of international character. Their aim should be to co-ordinate the policy pursued in the various centres in order to contribute towards the satisfactory working of the international gold standard system.

Moreover, they should endeavour to adapt their measures of credit regulation, as far as their domestic position permits, to any tendency towards an undue change in the state of general business activity. An expansion of general business activity of a kind which clearly cannot be permanently maintained, should lead central banks to introduce a bias towards credit restriction into the credit policy which they think fit to adopt, having regard to internal conditions in their own countries. On the other hand, an undue decline in general business activity in the world at large should lead them to introduce a bias towards relaxation.

In pursuing such a policy the central banks will have done what is in their power to reduce fluctuations in business activity and thereby also undue fluctuations in the purchasing power of gold.

6) With a view to arriving at an agreed interpretation of the data revealing the tendency of developments in general business activity, and at an agreed policy, central banks should consult together continuously, each central bank in case of difference of opinion, acting on its own judgment of the situation. The Bank for International Settlements constitutes an essential agency for central bank action designed to harmonise conflicting views and for joint consultation. This instrument should continue to be employed, as far as possible, for the realisation of the principles set forth in the present note. It should continuously examine the application of the principles of the working of the gold standard and study such modifications thereof as experience may prove desirable.

Agreement on the resolutions was reached by all governments represented at the Sub-Committee on Technical Monetary Problems, except that of the United States of America, which considered discussion of the question at this time premature, it being understood that the Federal Reserve Banks would be glad to confer at an opportune time with other central banks on questions of this character to the extent that they are compatible with national policies.

The sub-commission further took note of a report from the Sub-Committee on Technical Monetary Problems concerning the remaining subjects on its agenda, including a draft resolution submitted by the Irish Free State delegation. The report was as follows:

> The committee has not been able during the present session to complete its report on the section of the Annotated Agenda dealing with the gold exchange standard, with other methods of economising gold and with distribution of monetary reserves.
>
> As regards the gold exchange standard, the committee recommends that the Bank for International Settlements should as soon as possible proceed to a study of the question and particularly that it should examine to what extent it will prove possible to avoid certain of the defects which this system has revealed in the past.

12. The sub-commission was asked to clarify the permanent principles of monetary policy that ought to be pursued in future. It is satisfactory to note that it has achieved a measure of success in this task since it has proved possible to reach full agreement on certain important problems. This may be seen from the text of resolutions approved. The same unanimity was evident also in regard to the necessity of central bank co-operation. Finally it should be stated that the important task which the Bank for International Settlements must discharge in the future was fully recognized.

APPENDIX F

BRITISH IMPERIAL DECLARATION ON MONETARY POLICY[1]

At the Ottawa Conference the governments represented declared their view that a rise throughout the world in the general level of wholesale prices was in the highest degree desirable, and stated that they were anxious to co-operate with other nations in any practicable measures for raising wholesale prices. They agreed that a rise in prices could not be effected by monetary action alone, since various other factors which combined to bring about the present depression must also be modified or removed before a remedy is assured.

It was indicated that international action would be needed to remove the various non-monetary factors which were depressing the level of prices.

In the monetary sphere the primary line of action towards a rise in prices was stated to be the creation and maintenance within the limits of sound finance of such conditions as would assist in the revival of enterprise and trade, including low rates of interest and an abundance of short-term money. The inflationary creation of additional means of payment to finance public expenditure was deprecated, and an orderly monetary policy was demanded with safeguards to limit the scope of violent speculative movements of commodities and securities.

Since then the policy of the British Commonwealth has been directed to raising prices. The undersigned delegations note with satisfaction that this policy has been attended with an encouraging measure of success. For some months indeed it had to encounter obstacles arising from the continuance of a downward trend of gold prices, and during that period the results achieved were in the main limited to raising prices in Empire currencies relatively to gold prices. In the last few months the persistent adherence of the United Kingdom to the policy of

[1] Signed July 27 by the representatives of Great Britain, Canada, Australia, New Zealand, Union of South Africa, and India.

cheap and plentiful money has been increasingly effective under the more favourable conditions that have been created for the time being by the change of policy of the United States, and by the halt in the fall of gold prices.

Taking the whole period from June 29, 1932, just before the assembly of the Ottawa Conference, a rise in sterling wholesale prices has taken place of 12 per cent according to the "Economist" index. The rise in the sterling prices of primary products during the same period has been much more substantial, being in the neighborhood of 20 per cent.

The undersigned delegations are of opinion that the views they expressed at Ottawa as to the necessity of a rise in the price level still hold good and that it is of the greatest importance that this rise which has begun should continue. As to the ultimate level to be aimed at they do not consider it practicable to state this in precise terms. Any price level would be satisfactory which restores the normal activity of industry and employment, which ensures an economic return to the producer of primary commodities, and which harmonizes the burden of debts and fixed charges with economic capacity. It is important that the rise in prices should not be carried to such a pitch as to produce an inflated scale of profits and threaten a disturbance of equilibrium in the opposite direction. They therefore consider that the governments of the British Commonwealth should persist by all means in their power, whether monetary or economic, within the limits of sound finance in the policy of furthering the rise in wholesale prices until there is evidence that equilibrium has been re-established, and that thereupon they should take whatever measures are possible to stabilize the position thus attained.

With reference to the proposal which has been made from time to time for the expansion of government programmes of capital outlay, the British Commonwealth delegations consider that this is a matter which must be dealt with by each government in the light of its own experience and of its own conditions.

The Ottawa Conference declared that the ultimate aim of monetary policy must be the restoration of a satisfactory international monetary standard, having in mind, not merely stable exchange rates between all countries, but the deliberate management of the international standard in such a manner as to ensure the smooth and efficient working of international trade and finance. The principal conditions precedent to the re-establishment of any international monetary standard were stated, particularly a rise in the general level of commodity prices in the various countries to a height more in keeping with the level of costs, including the burden of debt and other fixed and semi-fixed charges, and the conference expressed its sense of the importance of securing and maintaining international co-operation with a view to avoiding, so far as may be found practicable, wide fluctuations in the purchasing power of the standard of value.

The undersigned delegations now reaffirm their view that the ultimate aim of monetary policy should be the restoration of a satisfactory international gold standard under which international co-operation would be secured and maintained with a view to avoiding, so far as may be found practicable, undue fluctuations in the purchasing power of gold. The problem with which the world is faced is to reconcile the stability of exchange rates with a reasonable measure of stability, not merely in the price level of a particular country, but in world prices. Effective action in this matter must largely depend on international co-operation, and in any further sessions of the World Economic and Monetary Conference this subject must have special prominence.

In the meantime the undersigned delegations recognize the importance of stability of exchange rates between the countries of the Empire in the interests of trade. This objective will be constantly kept in mind in determining their monetary policy, and its achievement will be aided by the pursuit of a common policy of raising price levels. Inter-Imperial stability of exchange rates is facilitated by the fact that the United Kingdom government has no commitments to other countries as regards the future management of sterling and retains complete freedom of action in this respect. The adherence of other countries to a policy on similar lines would make possible the attainment and maintenance of exchange stability over a still wider area.

Among the factors working for the economic recovery of the countries of the Commonwealth, special importance attaches to the decline in the rate of interest on long-term loans. The undersigned delegations note with satisfaction the progress which has been made in that direction as well as in the resumption of oversea lending by the London market. They agree that further advances on these lines will be beneficial as and when they can be made.

The undersigned delegations have agreed that they will recommend their governments to consult with one another from time to time on monetary and economic policy with a view to establishing their common purpose and to the framing of such measures as may conduce towards its achievement.

PRESIDENT ROOSEVELT'S RADIO ADDRESS
OF OCTOBER 22, 1933

It is three months since I have talked with the people of this country about our national problems; but during this period many things have happened, and I am glad to say that the major part of them have greatly helped the well-being of the average citizen.

Because, in every step which your government is taking we are thinking in terms of the average of you—in the old words, "the greatest good to the greatest number"—we, as reasonable people, cannot expect to bring definite benefits to every person or to every occupation or business, or industry or agriculture.

In the same way, no reasonable person can expect that in this short space of time, during which new machinery had to be not only put to work, but first set up, that every locality in every one of the forty-eight states of the country could share equally and simultaneously in the trend to better times.

The whole picture, however—the average of the whole territory from coast to coast, the average of the whole population of 120,000,000 people—shows to any person, willing to look, facts and action of which you and I can be proud.

In the early spring of this year there were actually and proportionately more people out of work in this country than in any other nation in the world. Fair estimates showed twelve or thirteen millions unemployed last March. Among those there were, of course, several millions who could be classed as normally unemployed—people who worked occasionally, when they felt like it, and others who preferred not to work at all.

It seems, therefore, fair to say that there were about 10,000,000 of our citizens who earnestly, and in many cases hungrily, were seeking work and could not get it. Of these, in the short space of a few months, I am convinced that at least 4,000,000 have been given employment—or, saying it another way, 40 per cent of those seeking work have found it.

That does not mean, my friends, that I am satisfied, or that you are satisfied that our work is ended. We have a long way to go, but we are on the way.

How are we constructing the edifice of recovery—the temple which, when completed, will no longer be a temple of money-changers or beggars, but rather a temple dedicated to and maintained for a greater social justice, a greater welfare for America —the habitation of a sound economic life?

We are building, stone by stone, the columns which will support that habitation. Those columns are many in number and though, for a moment, the progress of one column may disturb the progress on the pillar next to it, the work on all of them must proceed without let or hindrance.

We all know that immediate relief for the unemployed was the first essential of such a structure, and that is why I speak first of the fact that 300,000 young men have been given employment and are being given employment all through this winter in the Civilian Conservation Corps camps in almost every part of the nation.

So, too, we have, as you know, expended greater sums in co-operation with states and localities for work relief and home relief than ever before—sums which during the coming winter cannot be lessened for the very simple reason that though several million people have gone back to work, the necessities of those who have not yet obtained work is more severe than at this time last year.

Then we come to the relief that is being given to those who are in danger of losing their farms or their homes. New machinery had to be set up for farm credit and for home credit in every one of the 3,100 counties of the United States and every day that passes is saving homes and farms to hundreds of families.

I have publicly asked that foreclosures on farms and chattels and on homes be delayed until every mortgagor in the country shall have had full opportunity to take advantage of federal credit.

I make the further request which many of you know has already been made through the great federal credit organizations that, if there is any family in the United States about to lose its home or about to lose its chattels, that family should telegraph at once either to the Farm Credit Administration or the Home-Owners Loan Corporation in Washington requesting their help.

Two other great agencies are in full swing. The Reconstruction Finance Corporation continues to lend large sums to industry and finance with the definite objective of making easy the extending of credit to industry, commerce and finance.

The program of public works in three months has advanced to this point: Out of a total appropriated for public works of $3,300,000,000, $1,800,000,000 has already been allocated to federal projects of all kinds and literally in every part of the United States, and work on these is starting forward.

In addition $300,000,000 has been allocated to public works to be carried out by states, municipalities and private organizations, such as those undertaking slum clearance.

The balance of the public works money, nearly all of its intended for state or local projects, waits only on the presentation of proper projects by the states and localities themselves. Washington has the money and is waiting for the proper projects to which to allot it.

Another pillar in the making is the Agricultural Adjustment Administration. I have been amazed by the extraordinary degree of co-operation given to the government by the cotton farmers in the South, the wheat farmers of the West, the tobacco farmers of the Southeast, and I am confident that the corn hog farmers of the Middle West will come through in the same magnificent fashion.

The problem we seek to solve had been steadily getting worse for twenty years but during the last six months we have made more rapid progress than any nation has ever made in a like period of time.

It is true that in July farm commodity prices had been pushed up higher than they are today, but that push came in part from pure speculation by people who could not tell you the difference between wheat and rye, by people who had never seen cotton growing, by people who did not know that hogs were fed on corn—people who have no real interest in the farmer and his problems.

In spite, however, of the speculative reaction from the speculative advance, it seems to be well established that during the course of the year 1933 the farmers of the United States will receive 33 per cent more dollars for what they have produced than they received in the year 1932.

Put in another way, they will receive $400 in 1933 where they received $300 the year before. That, remember, is for the average of the country, for I have reports that some sections are not any better off than they were a year ago.

This applies among the major products, especially to cattle raising and the dairy industry. We are going after those problems as fast as we can.

I do not hesitate to say, in the simplest, clearest language of which I am capable, that, although the prices of many products of the farm have gone up and although many farm families are better off than they were last year, I am not satisfied either with the amount or the extent of the rise, and that it is definitely a part of our policy to increase the rise and to extend it to those products which have as yet felt no benefit. If we cannot do this one way we will do it another. Do it we will.

Standing beside the pillar of the farm—the AAA—is the pillar of industry—the NRA. Its object is to put industry and business workers into employment and to increase their purchasing power through increased wages.

It has abolished child labor. It has eliminated the sweatshop. It has ended 60 cents a week paid in some mills and 80 cents a week paid in some mines. The measure of the growth of this pillar lies in the total figures of re-employment, which I have already given you, and in the fact that re-employment is continuing and not stopping.

The secret of NRA is co-operation. That co-operation has been voluntarily given through the signing of the blanket codes and through the signing of specific codes which already include all of the greater industries of the nation.

In the vast majority of cases, in the vast majority of localities, the NRA has been given support in unstinted measure. We know that there are chiselers. At the bottom of every case of criticism and obstruction we have found some selfish interest, some private axe to grind.

Ninety per cent of complaints come from misconception. For

example, it has been said that NRA has failed to raise the price of wheat and corn and hogs; that NRA has not loaned enough money for local public works.

Of course, NRA has nothing whatsoever to do with the prices of farm products, nor with public works. It has to do only with industrial organization for economic planning to wipe out unfair practices and to create re-employment.

Even in the field of business and industry, NRA does not apply to the rural communities or to towns of under 2,500 population, except in so far as those towns contain factories or chain stores which come under a specific code.

It is also true that among the chislers to whom I have referred, there are not only the big chiselers but also petty chiselers who seek to make undue profit on untrue statements.

Let me cite to you the example of the salesman in a store in a large Eastern city who tried to justify the increase in the price of a cotton shirt from $1.50 to $2.50 by saying to the customer that it was due to the cotton processing tax. Actually in that shirt there was about one pound of cotton and the processing tax amounted to $4\frac{1}{4}$ cents on that pound of cotton.

At this point it is only fair that I should give credit to the sixty or seventy million people who live in the cities and larger towns of the nation for their understanding and their willingness to go along with the payment of even these small processing taxes, though they know full well that the proportion of the processing taxes on cotton goods and on foods paid for by city dwellers goes 100 per cent toward increasing the agricultural income of the farm dwellers of the land.

The last pillar of which I speak is that of the money of the country in the banks of the country. There are two simple facts.

First, the federal government is about to spend $1,000,000,000 as an immediate loan on the frozen or non-liquid assets of all banks closed since Jan. 1, 1933, giving a liberal appraisal to those assets. This money will be in the hands of the depositors as quickly as it is humanly possible to get it out.

Secondly, the government bank deposit insurance on all accounts up to $2,500 goes into effect on Jan. 1. We are now engaged in seeing to it that on or before that date the banking capital structure will be built up by the government to the point that the banks will be in sound condition when the insurance goes into effect.

Finally, I repeat what I have said on many occasions, that ever since last March the definite policy of the government has been to restore commodity price levels.

The object has been the attainment of such a level as will enable agriculture and industry once more to give work to the unemployed.

It has been to make possible the payment of public and private debts more nearly at the price level at which they were incurred.

It has been gradually to restore a balance in the price structure so that farmers may exchange their products for the products of industry on a fairer exchange basis.

It has been and is also the purpose to prevent prices from rising beyond the point necessary to attain these ends. The permanent welfare and security of every class of our people ultimately depends on our attainment of these purposes.

Obviously, and because hundreds of different kinds of crops and industrial occupations in the huge territory that makes up this nation are involved, we cannot reach the goal in only a few months. We may take one year or two years or three years.

No one who considers the plain facts of our situation believes that commodity prices, especially agricultural prices, are high enough yet.

Some people are putting the cart before the horse. They want a permanent revaluation of the dollar first. It is the government's policy to restore the price level first. I would not know, and no one else could tell, just what the permanent valuation of the dollar will be. To guess at a permanent gold valuation now would certainly require later changes caused by later facts.

When we have restored the price level, we shall seek to establish and maintain a dollar which will not change its purchasing and debt-paying power during the succeeding generation. I said that in my message to the American delegation in London last July. And I say it now once more.

Because of conditions in this country and because of events beyond our control in other parts of the world, it becomes increasingly important to develop and apply the further measures which may be necessary from time to time to control the gold value of our own dollar at home.

Our dollar is now altogether too greatly influenced by the accidents of international trade, by the internal policies of other nations and by political disturbance in other continents.

Therefore the United States must take firmly in its own hands the control of the gold value of our dollar. This is necessary in order to prevent dollar disturbances from swinging us away from our ultimate goal, namely, the continued recovery of our commodity prices.

As a further effective means to this end, I am going to establish a government market for gold in the United States. Therefore, under the clearly defined authority of existing law, I am authorizing the Reconstruction Finance Corporation to buy gold newly mined in the United States at prices to be determined from time to time after consultation with the Secretary of the Treasury and the President. Whenever necessary to the end in view, we shall also buy or sell gold in the world market.

My aim in taking this step is to establish and maintain continuous control.

This is a policy and not an expedient.

It is not to be used merely to offset a temporary fall in prices. We are thus continuing to move toward a managed currency.

You will recall the dire predictions made last spring by those who did not agree with our common policies of raising prices by direct means. What actually happened stood out in sharp contrast with those predictions. Government credit is high, prices have risen in part.

Doubtless, prophets of evil still exist in our midst. But government credit will be maintained and a sound currency will accompany a rise in the American commodity price level.

I have told you tonight the story of our steady but sure work in building our common recovery. In my promises to you, both before and after March 4, I made two things plain—first, that I pledged no miracles, and second, that I would do my best.

I thank you for your patience and your faith. Our troubles will not be over tomorrow, but we are on our way and we are headed in the right direction.

INDEX

Agricultural Adjustment Administration, 100, 124
Anti-hoarding order, 41

Bank for International Settlements, 31, 88
Banking crisis in United States, 37
Belgium, 13, 93
Bimetalism, 30, 49
Bonnet, G., 71, 94
British Dominions, 79, 96, 99
British Imperial policy, 96-99
Brussels Conference, 5
Budgetary balance, 31, 75, 78-79

Central banking, 24, 88, 89, 176
Commercial policy, 86, 90
Compensated dollar, 21, 113-15, 131
Cox, J. M., 70
Currency depreciation, 6, 26, 42, 69, 99, 109, 119-26. *See also* frontispiece
Customs truce, 64
Czechoslovakia, 7, 72

Day, E. E., 16
Debts, private, 87, 149-51
Debts, war, 32, 65

Emergency Banking Act, 38
Exchange Equalization Account, 11, 67

Federal Reserve system, 41, 44, 47, 53, 89, 100
Foreign exchange, 10-12, 24, 26, 40, 66-70, 148-49
France, 22, 66, 67, 73, 78, 117
Fraser, L., 16

Genoa Conference, 5
Germany, 7

Great Britain, 6, 23, 66, 79, 116, 132
Greenbacks, 48, 100, 129
Gold Bloc, 92-95
Gold clause, 51
Gold Delegation of the League of Nations, 22, 31
Gold in circulation, 43
Gold points, 9
Gold, price of, 102, 108
Gold purchase plan, 104, Ch. VI
Gold standard, 5, 7, 17-26, 30, 37, 81, 135-43

Herriot, E., 55, 65, 66, 155
Hull, C., 86

International monetary system, 10, 22, 131
India, 13
Italy, 22, 73, 117

Japan, 6, 72, 116, 119
Jung, G., 55, 156

Keynes, J. M., 61

Lausanne Conference, 3, 14
League of Nations, 16, 60
Legal tender powers, 50
Lindahl, E., 120

MacDonald, R., 55, 65, 66, 154
Managed currency, 19-20. *See also* Compensated dollar
Moley, R., 63, 82
Monetary standard position, 8
Monetary uncertainty, 73-74, 128-30

National Recovery Administration, 100, 124
Netherlands, The, 13, 22, 72, 80

Open market operations, 47, 75, 100

Pittman, Senator, 47, 84, 88, 159
Poland, 93
Preparatory Commission of Experts, Ch. II, 76
Price-cost adjustment, 23-25, 97, 104
Price-raising, 26-29, 32, 46, 52-54, 56, 59, 70-80, 110-13
Price stability, 18, 19, 21, 83-85, 96, 131
Price structure, 21, 118, 124
Prices, effect of currency depreciation on, 119-26

Reconstruction Finance Corporation, 105, 111

Reflation, 28
Roosevelt, President, 52, 55-60, 62, 69, 82, 84, 103, 154-56

Sweden, 77, 116, 120
Switzerland, 73, 80
Silver, 49, 59, 84, 143, 173
Sterling area, 98

Thomas amendment, 47-54, 101

United States, 13, 22, Ch. III, 66, 74, 76, 99-106, 117, 123

Warren, G. F., 115, 118
Williams, J. H., 16
World Monetary and Economic Conference, 14, 16, Chs. II and IV

PUBLICATIONS OF THE BROOKINGS INSTITUTION*

INSTITUTE OF ECONOMICS SERIES

(1.) GERMANY'S CAPACITY TO PAY.
> By Harold G. Moulton and Constantine E. McGuire. 384 pp. 1923. $2.50.

(2.) RUSSIAN DEBTS AND RUSSIAN RECONSTRUCTION.
> By Leo Pasvolsky and Harold G. Moulton. 247 pp. 1924. $2.50.

(3.) MAKING THE TARIFF IN THE UNITED STATES.
> By Thomas Walker Page. 281 pp. 1924. $3.

(4.) AMERICAN AGRICULTURE AND THE EUROPEAN MARKET.
> By Edwin G. Nourse. 333 pp. 1924. $2.50.

(5.) SUGAR IN RELATION TO THE TARIFF.
> By Philip G. Wright. 312 pp. 1924. $2.50.

(6.) MINERS' WAGES AND THE COST OF COAL.
> By Isador Lubin. 316 pp. 1924. Out of print.

(7.) THE REPARATION PLAN.
> By Harold G. Moulton. 325 pp. 1924. $2.50.

(8). THE FRENCH DEBT PROBLEM.
> By Harold G. Moulton and Cleona Lewis. 459 pp. 1925. $2.

(9.) THE RUHR-LORRAINE INDUSTRIAL PROBLEM.
> By Guy Greer. 328 pp. 1925. $2.50.

(10.) THE CASE OF BITUMINOUS COAL.
> By Walton H. Hamilton and Helen R. Wright. 310 pp. 1925. $2.50.

(11.) INTEREST RATES AND STOCK SPECULATION.
> By Richard N. Owens and Charles O. Hardy. 221 pp. rev. ed. 1930. $2.50.

(12.) THE FEDERAL INTERMEDIATE CREDIT SYSTEM.
> By Claude L. Benner. 375 pp. 1926. Out of print.

(13.) THE TARIFF ON WOOL.
> By Mark A. Smith. 350 pp. 1926. $2.50.

*The parentheses indicate that the volume itself does not carry the number since it was given subsequent to publication.

(14.) THE CATTLE INDUSTRY AND THE TARIFF.
   By Lynn Ramsay Edminster. 331 pp. 1926. $2.50.
(15.) THE COAL MINERS' STRUGGLE FOR INDUSTRIAL STATUS.
   By Arthur E. Suffern. 462 pp. 1926. $2.50.
(16.) TAX-EXEMPT SECURITIES AND THE SURTAX.
   By Charles O. Hardy. 216 pp. 1926. $2.
(17.) WORLD WAR DEBT SETTLEMENTS.
   By Harold G. Moulton and Leo Pasvolsky. 448 pp. 1926. $2.
(18.) FINANCING THE LIVESTOCK INDUSTRY.
   By Forrest M. Larmer. 327 pp. 1926. $2.50.
(19.) ITALY'S INTERNATIONAL ECONOMIC POSITION.
   By Constantine E. McGuire. 588 pp. 1926. $3.
(20.) WORKERS' HEALTH AND SAFETY: A STATISTICAL PROGRAM.
   By Robert Morse Woodbury. 207 pp. 1927. $2.50.
(21.) THE INTERNATIONAL ACCOUNTS.
   By Cleona Lewis. 170 pp. 1927. $2.
(22.) INDUSTRIAL PROSPERITY AND THE FARMER.
   By Russell C. Engberg. 286 pp. 1927. $2.50.
(23.) THE LEGAL STATUS OF AGRICULTURAL CO-OPERATION.
   By Edwin G. Nourse. 555 pp. 1927. $3.
(24.) AMERICAN LOANS TO GERMANY.
   By Robert R. Kuczynski. 378 pp. 1927. $3.
(25.) THE BRITISH COAL DILEMMA.
   By Isador Lubin and Helen Everett. 370 pp. 1927. $2.50.
(26.) THE TARIFF ON ANIMAL AND VEGETABLE OILS.
   By Philip G. Wright. 347 pp. 1928. $2.50.
(27.) A WAY OF ORDER FOR BITUMINOUS COAL.
   By Walton H. Hamilton and Helen R. Wright. 365 pp. 1928. $2.50.
(28.) ECONOMIC NATIONALISM OF THE DANUBIAN STATES.
   By Leo Pasvolsky. 609 pp. 1928. $3.
(29.) THE BALANCE OF BIRTHS AND DEATHS. Vol. I, Western and Northern Europe.
   By Robert R. Kuczynski. 140 pp. 1928. Out of print.

(30.) LABOR AND INTERNATIONALISM.
    By Lewis L. Lorwin. 682 pp. 1929. $3.
(31.) THE MEXICAN AGRARIAN REVOLUTION.
    By Frank Tannenbaum. 543 pp. 1929. $3.
(32.) THE TARIFF ON IRON AND STEEL.
    By Abraham Berglund and Philip G. Wright. 240
    pp. 1929. $3.
(33.) THE ST. LAWRENCE NAVIGATION AND POWER PROJ-
    ECT.
    By Harold G. Moulton, Charles S. Morgan, and
    Adah L. Lee. 675 pp. 1929. $4.
(34.) RAILROAD PURCHASING AND THE BUSINESS CYCLE.
    By John E. Partington. 309 pp. 1929. $3.
(35.) HAND-TO-MOUTH BUYING: A STUDY IN THE ORGANI-
    ZATION, PLANNING, AND STABILIZATION OF
    TRADE.
    By Leverett S. Lyon. 487 pp. 1929. $4.
(36.) UNEMPLOYMENT INSURANCE IN GERMANY.
    By Mollie Ray Carroll. 137 pp. 1929. $2.50.
(37.) INTERNATIONAL CONTROL OF RAW MATERIALS.
    By Benjamin Bruce Wallace and Lynn Ramsay
    Edminster. 479 pp. 1930. $3.50.
(38.) BIRTH REGISTRATION AND BIRTH STATISTICS IN
    CANADA.
    By Robert Kuczynski. 219 pp. 1930. $3.
(39.) BULGARIA's ECONOMIC POSITION.
    By Leo Pasvolsky. 409 pp. 1930. $3.
40. THE CO-OPERATIVE MARKETING OF LIVESTOCK.
    By Edwin G. Nourse and Joseph G. Knapp. 486 pp.
    1931. $3.50.
41. BANKERS' PROFITS FROM GERMAN LOANS.
    By Robert R. Kuczynski. 228 pp. 1932. $1.75.
42. THE CUBAN SITUATION AND OUR TREATY RELA-
    TIONS.
    By Philip G. Wright. 208 pp. 1931. $2.50.
43. THE BALANCE OF BIRTHS AND DEATHS. Vol. II, East-
    ern and Southern Europe.
    By Robert R. Kuczynski. 170 pp. 1931. $2.

44. JAPAN: AN ECONOMIC AND FINANCIAL APPRAISAL.
    By Harold G. Moulton with the collaboration of
    Junichi Ko. 645 pp. 1931. $4.

45. CREDIT POLICIES OF THE FEDERAL RESERVE SYSTEM.
    By Charles O. Hardy. 374 pp. 1932. $2.50.

46. WAR DEBTS AND WORLD PROSPERITY.
    By Harold G. Moulton and Leo Pasvolsky. 498 pp.
    1932. $3.

47. ADVERTISING ALLOWANCES: A PHASE OF THE PRICE-
    MAKING PROCESS.
    By Leverett S. Lyon. 125 pp. 1932. $1.

48. TEN YEARS OF FEDERAL INTERMEDIATE CREDITS.
    By Frieda Baird and Claude L. Benner. 416 pp. 1933.
    $2.75.

49. SILVER: AN ANALYSIS OF FACTORS AFFECTING ITS
    PRICE.
    By Y. S. Leong. 168 pp. 1933. $2.

50. THE AMERICAN FEDERATION OF LABOR: HISTORY,
    POLICIES, AND PROSPECTS.
    By Lewis L. Lorwin. 573 pp. 1933. $2.75.

51. THE BRITISH ATTACK ON UNEMPLOYMENT.
    By Isador Lubin and A. C. C. Hill, Jr. (In press.)

52. CURRENT MONETARY ISSUES.
    By Leo Pasvolsky. 192 pp. 1933. $1.50.

53. THE ECONOMICS OF FREE DEALS: WITH SUGGES-
    TIONS FOR CODE-MAKING UNDER THE NRA.
    By Leverett S. Lyon. (In press.)

INSTITUTE FOR GOVERNMENT RESEARCH SERIES
Studies in Administration

(1.) THE SYSTEM OF FINANCIAL ADMINISTRATION OF
    GREAT BRITAIN.
    By W. F. Willoughby, W. W. Willoughby, and S.
    M. Lindsay. 362 pp. 1917. $3.

(2.) THE BUDGET: A TRANSLATION.
    By René Stourm. 619 pp. 1917. $4.

(3.) THE PROBLEM OF A NATIONAL BUDGET.
    By W. F. Willoughby. 220 pp. 1918. Out of print.

LIST OF PUBLICATIONS

(4.) THE MOVEMENT FOR BUDGETARY REFORM IN THE STATES.

By W. F. Willoughby. 254 pp. 1918. $3.

(5.) THE CANADIAN BUDGETARY SYSTEM.

By H. C. Villard and W. W. Willoughby. 379 pp. 1918. $3.

(6.) ORGANIZED EFFORTS FOR THE IMPROVEMENT OF METHODS OF ADMINISTRATION IN THE UNITED STATES.

By Gustavus A. Weber. 391 pp. 1919. $3.

(7.) TEACHERS' PENSION SYSTEMS IN THE UNITED STATES.

By Paul Studensky. 460 pp. 1920. $3.

(8.) THE FEDERAL SERVICE: A STUDY OF THE SYSTEM OF PERSONNEL ADMINISTRATION OF THE UNITED STATES GOVERNMENT.

By Lewis Mayers. 607 pp. 1922. $5.

(9.) THE REORGANIZATION OF THE ADMINISTRATIVE BRANCH OF THE NATIONAL GOVERNMENT.

By W. F. Willoughby. 298 pp. 1923. Out of print.

(10.) THE DEVELOPMENT OF NATIONAL ADMINISTRATIVE ORGANIZATION IN THE UNITED STATES.

By Lloyd M. Short. 514 pp. 1923. $5.

(11.) THE STATISTICAL WORK OF THE NATIONAL GOVERNMENT.

By Laurence F. Schmeckebier. 574 pp. 1925. $5.

(12.) MANUAL OF ACCOUNTING AND REPORTING FOR THE OPERATING SERVICES OF THE NATIONAL GOVERNMENT.

By Henry P. Seidemann. 399 pp. 1926. $5.

(13.) THE NATIONAL GOVERNMENT AND PUBLIC HEALTH.

By James A. Tobey. 423 pp. 1926. $3.

(14.) THE NATIONAL BUDGET SYSTEM, WITH SUGGESTIONS FOR ITS IMPROVEMENT.

By W. F. Willoughby. 343 pp. 1927. $3.

(15.) THE DEPARTMENT OF JUSTICE OF THE UNITED STATES.

By Albert Langeluttig. 318 pp. 1927. $3.

(16.) THE LEGAL STATUS AND FUNCTIONS OF THE GENERAL ACCOUNTING OFFICE.
    By W. F. Willoughby. 193 pp. 1927. $3.

(17.) THE PROBLEM OF INDIAN ADMINISTRATION.
    By Lewis Meriam and Associates. 872 pp. 1928. $5.

(18.) THE DISTRICT OF COLUMBIA: ITS GOVERNMENT AND ADMINISTRATION.
    By Laurence F. Schmeckebier. 943 pp. 1928. $5.

(19.) THE DEVELOPMENT OF GOVERNMENTAL FOREST CONTROL IN THE UNITED STATES.
    By Jenks Cameron. 471 pp. 1928. $3.

(20.) MANUAL OF ACCOUNTING, REPORTING, AND BUSINESS PROCEDURE FOR THE TERRITORIAL GOVERNMENT OF HAWAII.
    By Henry P. Seidemann. 570 pp. 1928. $5.

(21.) THE GOVERNMENT AND ADMINISTRATION OF GERMANY.
    By Frederick F. Blachly and Miriam E. Oatman. 770 pp. 1928. $5.

(22.) GROUP REPRESENTATION BEFORE CONGRESS.
    By E. Pendleton Herring. 309 pp. 1929. $3.

(23.) REGISTRATION OF VOTERS IN THE UNITED STATES.
    By Joseph P. Harris. 390 pp. 1929. $3.

(24.) THE GOVERNMENT AND ADMINISTRATION OF THE DISTRICT OF COLUMBIA: SUGGESTIONS FOR CHANGE.
    By Laurence F. Schmeckebier and W. F. Willoughby. 187 pp. 1929. $2.

25. FINANCIAL CONDITION AND OPERATION OF THE NATIONAL GOVERNMENT, 1921-1930.
    By W. F. Willoughby. 234 pp. 1931. $3.

26. STATE CENTRALIZATION IN NORTH CAROLINA.
    By Paul V. Betters (editor). 261 pp. 1932. $2.

27. ELECTION ADMINISTRATION IN THE UNITED STATES.
    By Joseph Harris. (In press.)

LIST OF PUBLICATIONS

Principles of Administration

(1.) PRINCIPLES GOVERNING THE RETIREMENT OF PUBLIC EMPLOYEES.
By Lewis Meriam. 477 pp. 1918. Out of print.

(2.) PRINCIPLES OF GOVERNMENT PURCHASING.
By Arthur G. Thomas. 275 pp. 1919. $3.

(3.) PRINCIPLES OF GOVERNMENT ACCOUNTING AND REPORTING.
By Francis Oakey. 561 pp. 1921. Out of print.

(4.) PRINCIPLES OF PUBLIC PERSONNEL ADMINISTRATION.
By Arthur W. Procter. 244 pp. 1921. $3.

(5.) PRINCIPLES OF PUBLIC ADMINISTRATION.
By W. F. Willoughby. 720 pp. 1927. $5.

(6.) PRINCIPLES OF JUDICIAL ADMINISTRATION.
By W. F. Willoughby. 662 pp. 1929. $5.

Service Monographs of the United States Government

1. Geological Survey. 163 pp. 1918. Out of print.
2. Reclamation Service. 177 pp. 1919. Out of print.
3. Bureau of Mines. 162 pp. 1922. $1.
4. Alaskan Engineering Commission. 124 pp. 1922. $1.
5. Tariff Commission. 71 pp. 1922. $1.
6. Federal Board for Vocational Education. 74 pp. 1922. $1.
7. Federal Trade Commission. 80 pp. 1922. $1.
8. Steamboat-Inspection Service. 130 pp. 1922. $1.
9. Weather Bureau. 87 pp. 1922. $1.
10. Public Health Service. 298 pp. 1923. $2.
11. National Park Service. 172 pp. 1922. $1.
12. Employees' Compensation Commission. 86 pp. 1922. $1.
13. General Land Office. 224 pp. 1923. $1.50.
14. Bureau of Education. 157 pp. 1923. $1.
15. Bureau of Navigation. 124 pp. 1923. $1.
16. Coast and Geodetic Survey. 107 pp. 1923. $1.
17. Federal Power Commission. 126 pp. 1923. $1.
18. Interstate Commerce Commission. 169 pp. 1923. Out of print.
19. Railroad Labor Board. 83 pp. 1923. $1.

20. Division of Conciliation. 37 pp. 1923. $1.
21. Children's Bureau. 83 pp. 1925. $1.
22. Women's Bureau. 31 pp. 1923. $1.
23. Office of the Supervising Architect. 138 pp. 1923. $1.
24. Bureau of Pensions. 111 pp. 1923. $1.
25. Bureau of Internal Revenue. 270 pp. 1923. $1.50.
26. Bureau of Public Roads. 123 pp. 1923. $1.
27. Office of the Chief of Engineers. 166 pp. 1923. $1.
28. United States Employment Service. 130 pp. 1923. $1.
29. Bureau of Foreign and Domestic Commerce. 180 pp. 1924. $1.
30. Bureau of Immigration. 247 pp. 1924. $1.50.
31. Patent Office. 127 pp. 1924. Out of print.
32. Office of Experiment Stations. 178 pp. 1924. $1.
33. Customs Service. 191 pp. 1924. Out of print.
34. Federal Farm Loan Bureau. 160 pp. 1924. $1.
35. Bureau of Standards. 299 pp. 1925. $2.
36. Government Printing Office. 143 pp. 1925. $1.
37. Bureau of the Mint. 90 pp. 1926. $1.
38. Office of the Comptroller of the Currency. 84 pp. 1926. $1.
39. Naval Observatory. 101 pp. 1926. $1.
40. Lighthouse Service. 158 pp. 1926. $1.
41. Bureau of Animal Industry. 190 pp. 1927. $1.50.
42. Hydrographic Office. 112 pp. 1926. $1.
43. Bureau of Naturalization. 108 pp. 1926. $1.
44. Panama Canal. 413 pp. 1927. $2.50.
45. Medical Department of the Army. 161 pp. 1927. $1.50.
46. General Accounting Office. 215 pp. 1927. $1.50.
47. Bureau of Plant Industry. 121 pp. 1927. $1.
48. Office of Indian Affairs. 591 pp. 1927. $3.
49. United States Civil Service Commission. 153 pp. 1928. $1.50.
50. Food, Drug and Insecticide Administration. 134 pp. 1928. $1.50.
51. Coast Guard. 265 pp. 1929. $1.50.
52. Bureau of Chemistry and Soils. 218 pp. 1928. $1.50.
53. Bureau of the Census. 224 pp. 1929. $1.50.
54. Bureau of Biological Survey. 339 pp. 1929. $2.
55. Bureau of Dairy Industry. 74 pp. 1929. $1.50.

56. Bureau of Engraving and Printing. 111 pp. 1929. $1.50.
57. Bureau of Prohibition. 333 pp. 1929. $2.
58. Forest Service. 268 pp. 1930. $2.
59. Plant Quarantine and Control Administration. 198 pp. 1930. $1.50.
60. Bureau of Entomology. 177 pp. 1930. $1.50.
61. Aeronautics Branch: Department of Commerce. 147 pp. 1930. $1.50.
62. Bureau of Home Economics. 95 pp. 1930. $1.50.
63. United States Shipping Board. 338 pp. 1931. $2.50.
64. The Personnel Classification Board. 160 pp. 1931. $1.50.
65. The Federal Radio Commission. 159 pp. 1932. $1.50.
66. The Veterans' Administration. (In press.)

MISCELLANEOUS SERIES

PORTO RICO AND ITS PROBLEMS.
By Victor S. Clark and Associates. 707 pp. 1930. $5.
STEPHEN J. FIELD: CRAFTSMAN OF THE LAW.
By Carl Brent Swisher. 473 pp. 1930. $4.
THE SPIRIT OF '76 AND OTHER ESSAYS.
By Carl Becker, J. M. Clark, and William E. Dodd. 135 pp. 1927. $1.50.
ESSAYS ON RESEARCH IN THE SOCIAL SCIENCES.
By W. F. G. Swann and others. 194 pp. 1931. $2.
THE SOCIETY OF NATIONS: ITS ORGANIZATION AND CONSTITUTIONAL DEVELOPMENT.
By Felix Morley. 678 pp. 1932. $3.50.
THE AMERICAN TRANSPORTATION PROBLEM.
By Harold G. Moulton and Associates. 895 pp. $3.

PAMPHLETS

No. 1. RECENT GROWTH OF THE ELECTRIC LIGHT AND POWER INDUSTRY.
By Charles O. Hardy. 53 pp. 1929. 50 cents.
No. 2. FIRST MORTGAGES IN URBAN REAL ESTATE FINANCE.
By John H. Gray and George W. Terborgh. 69 pp. 1929. 50 cents.

LIST OF PUBLICATIONS

No. 3. THE ABSORPTION OF THE UNEMPLOYED BY AMERICAN INDUSTRY.

By Isador Lubin. 36 pp. 1929. 50 cents.

No. 4. SOME TRENDS IN THE MARKETING OF CANNED FOODS.

By Leverett S. Lyon. 57 pp. 1929. 50 cents.

No. 5. THE FECUNDITY OF NATIVE AND FOREIGN-BORN WOMEN IN NEW ENGLAND.

By Joseph J. Spengler. 63 pp. 1930. 50 cents.

No. 6. SOURCES OF COAL AND TYPES OF STOKERS AND BURNERS USED BY ELECTRIC PUBLIC UTILITY POWER PLANTS.

By William H. Young. 83 pp. 1930. 50 cents.

No. 7. FEDERAL SERVICES TO MUNICIPAL GOVERNMENTS.

By Paul V. Betters, 100 pp. 1931. 50 cents.

No. 8. REORGANIZATION OF THE FINANCIAL ADMINISTRATION OF THE DOMINICAN REPUBLIC.

By Taylor G. Addison. 105 pp. 1931. 50 cents.

No. 9. ADVISORY ECONOMIC COUNCILS.

By Lewis L. Lorwin, 84 pp. 1931. 50 cents.

No. 10. UNEMPLOYMENT INSURANCE IN AUSTRIA.

By Mollie Ray Carroll. 52 pp. 1932. 50 cents.